Peter's School, Littleover

St. Peter's Church School, Littleover
1845 - 1945

By Peter Brown

*Aiming to provide a high standard
of education within a stimulating and
caring Christian environment.*

ISBN 0-9547637-0-X

Further copies can be obtained from the publisher
or St. Peter's Church of England (Aided) Junior School,
Church Street, Littleover, Derby DE23 6GD.

Published by:

Peter Brown,
17 Gisborne Close,
Mickleover, Derby DE3 9LU.
Printed by The Reliance Press Ltd., Mansfield, Nottinghamshire.

This book is dedicated to the late Alice Yardley,
Lecturer in Primary Education at
Nottingham Training College.
A true friend who gave encouragement
and support to my ideas.

Acknowledgments

No amount of research into a school's history can be achieved without the help of those running it at the present time. A pleasant surprise after approaching Shaun Miles, the headteacher of St Peter's Church School, was the amount of material that was still available for me to study. With his support and that of his staff, particularly Kate Vance the school caretaker, who willingly scrambled in a dusty loft to retrieve school records, I have been able to search the very heart of the school.

I have received tremendous help with other research from family and friends, particularly my sister Sheila. Michael Bowden and Bill Elbers have helped in my research and Alwyn Johnson provided me with a personal account of Derby Diocesan Training College along with photographs. Dorothy Glynn, Sheila Clark and Hazel Warhurst have been kind enough to correct any grammatical howlers and guided me through the contents of the book, Dorothy also allowing me to use a small library of books on education from her own collection. Thanks to former pupils Peter Ekins, Brenda Jinks, (who married another pupil) Graham Luke, John Shepley, Doreen Smith and Eddie Townsend. Last but not least I thank my wife Ann who has shown extreme patience and helped in the research at the Local Study Library, County Records Office in Matlock and accompanied me over many weeks at The Magic Attic in Swadlincote, reading hundreds of newspapers. Their help and advice has been invaluable.

St. Peter's
CHURCH OF ENGLAND (AIDED)
Junior School
Headteacher: Mr. S. T. Miles B.Ed.(Hons).A.S.M.T.C.N.P.Q.H. Tel: 01332 767158
DERBY CITY COUNCIL   Q   Diocese of Derby

Author's Notes

The history of St Peter's Church of England School at Littleover is long and distinguished and I have based the founding of the school from the date the Trust Deed for the land was signed, May 20th 1845. This was twenty five years before the first Education Act in this country in 1870. The school had to produce a very difficult balancing act to survive, depending mostly on the charges made to the working class people in the village and the dedicated work put in by the people from St Peter's Church.

Government school inspectors also had a great influence, particularly in the granting of aid based on attendance figures. However it was through other inspectors in the country, such as Matthew Arnold, that compulsory education became a reality.

St Peter's progress came from three exceptional headmasters before the school reached its centenary. All stamped their mark on improving the standards and all had a love of music and a religious belief that transferred to the children.

Another interesting aspect in the growth of the school was the building extensions, the first two attached to the original building on Church Street. The third, in 1912 was separated by a corridor from the main block. The major complex of classrooms to the north was built just before the start of the Second World War which caused something of a controversy in the village. The church of course has always supported the school from its outset and a great deal of thanks must go to the vicars who acted as the chairman of the school managers, working hard to raise the necessary capital. Many former pupils pay tribute to the church for giving them a grounding in their religious knowledge.

As the records of the school go back to its foundation in 1845 I decided to include daily school life with other important events that were taking place at that time, both locally and nationally.

I was a pupil at the school in a difficult period, the end of the Second World War, and I became one of the first pupils to experience a radical change in education, the 1944 Education Act.

My personal thoughts on the school, which I admit are somewhat dim, come at the end of the book. A second book *Mickleover Born & Bred* follows this, which concentrates more on living through the period of war and personal memories from my contemporaries attending two schools in Littleover, St Peter's and the County Secondary School on Pastures Hill.

ILLUSTRATIONS

Author and Year 5 discuss school documents in 2004.

CONTENTS

CHAPTER ONE

LITTLEOVER LEARNING!

1845 – 1895

At the time of the Domesday Survey in 1086, William the Conqueror had given the extensive manor of Mickleover to the Benedictine Abbey at Burton-on-Trent. This included the settlements at Littleover, Findern and Potlock (near Radbourne). Although they all possessed chapels they were still dependent on the mother church at Mickleover.

Littleover was tied to Mickleover for the next seven hundred and eighty years so it is not surprising that the larger manor made an attempt to form a school as early as 1765 in the chancel of the parish church. It was the Nonconformist churches who first provided charitable instruction; Quaker Joseph Lancaster being at the forefront with his school at Southwark, London. He was attacked in 1792 by Sarah Trimmer, well known in the Tory establishment for her *Reflections upon the Education of Children in Charity Schools,* where she states. "The children of the poor should not be educated in such a manner as to set them above the occupations of humble life, or so as to make them uncomfortable among their equals."

The Anglican Church in 1811 founded "The National Society for the Education of the Poor in the Principles of the Established Church." The society established monitorial schools, a system where the master taught a group of 'monitors' (older pupils) who then followed this by reproducing the same lesson for the younger children. The education was mechanical and somewhat uninspired, concentrating on the three 'Rs' and lessons in religion. Dr. Robert Bell established parish schools and there was a Bell School in Orchard Street, Derby, in 1812.

A sermon was given in St. Paul's Cathedral by the Rev. Dr Herbert Marsh, Professor of Divinity at Cambridge, in which he asserted that only the established church could properly discharge education with the notion that, "national education must be conducted on the principles of the national religion."

The response to this was immediate with accusations of Anglican hypocrisy, bigotry, narrow mindedness and a lack of concern for the poor, disadvantaged and the vulnerable. Other religious denominations appeared   offering some form of education, but the ideas of Joseph

Lancaster and the Anglican support for The National Society gained the wider following.

A Factory Act of 1833 helped those who worked in the textile industry by no longer allowing the employment of children under nine years of age and limiting those aged nine to thirteen to nine hours a day, six days a week, with two hours for schooling in the factory. For the first time appointed inspectors were included under the Act to establish these schools but the factories never carried this out with any conviction. Factory inspectors helped by presenting a report on education which led to the formation of the Committee of Council for Education and the appointment of two inspectors for education. This was to incorporate church schools but eventually separate inspectors for the Church of England, Nonconformist and Catholic Schools were introduced.

The State also laid down a grant of £20,000 in 1833 to assist the National Society and a Free Church group with the building of schools. This was increased in 1839 when a Privy Council Committee set up the granting of money for school building, the appointment of Government inspectors and the beginning of a State Training College, open to all sects.

Dames' Schools which were operating all over the country at that time were mainly run by unmarried women with a little education, provided in a room in their own homes. The children received only the rudiments of education based on the Bible, the Dame's main task was to teach them their trade and fill her quotas. A committee of St. Peter's Church in Littleover decided to apply to the National Society for grants in 1842 to aid the building of a new school.

According to the 1841 Census, Littleover was a small community of 497 people, most of them farmers and farm labourers and the Enumerators list names a Thomas Manifold, as a schoolmaster. He had attempted to hold a daily school connected to the church in a hired room but as he was unable to make a living the school was closed.

The Curate at St. Peter's, the Rev. J. G. Howard, wrote to the National Society on October 6th 1842: "I beg to address you on the subject of establishing a school in connection with the Church of England in the parish of Littleover, near Derby, of which I am the Curate." He describes the population of the village and the lack of previous efforts to bring regular schooling. He continues, "My present object is to procure the erection of a school room,

Derby Oct 8th 1842.

Rev. Sir,

I beg to address you on the subject of establishing a school in connection with the Church of England in the parish of Littleover, near Derby, of which I am the Curate.

The population is 500. A school has long been taught by a woman who is a member of the Baptist Society in the village; & upon the removal of the master of a school lately supported in the Church on account of his being unable to make Littleover, a school was started in the Wesleyan chapel. So that had the Baptists & Wesleyans have a school &c.

My present object is to procure the erection of a school room, with a cottage for a master

attached to it; & that will be by any means found possible; & likewise to procure an annual grant towards small towards the payment of a master. This step seems necessary to the efficiency of the Church in this village. Could we derive any assistance toward the carrying out of this object from your valuable society? The chief Salvation would be a grant towards the Masters salary. which if anything only from his own exertions would be small. for the first year at least.

I have the honour to be
Sir,
Your obedient servant
G. Howard
Curate of Littleover.

N.B. My address is "Normanton near Derby."

Curate Howard's first letter to the National Society.

3

with a cottage for the master attached to it if that were by any means found possible; likewise to procure an annual grant however small towards the payment of a master."

His next task, in March 1844, was to fill in the relevant application form which included all the dimensions of a new school building and all the costs of the undertaking, £274.10s.0d (£274.50p). He also states on the form that the nonconformist chapels in the village were keen to become involved in education; the Methodists and Baptists already managed Sunday Schools. The form also highlights that school attendance could be increased by including the population of Mickleover which had a school containing about twenty children and the nearby parish of Normanton which had no school at all.

Littleover was in the diocese of Lichfield which meant the completed form was dispatched to the Bishop for him to endorse on March 27th before being forwarded to the National Society in London.

Two months later the curate wrote to the Society thanking them for their promise of a grant of £40 towards the establishment of the National School. He did so without the knowledge of the Trustees but he informed them that the Privy Council Committee had pledged a further £70. There now appears to be a shortfall; when added together the money raised totalled £192.12s.0d (£192.60p) – £40 from the National Society, £70 from the Privy Council and a possible £82.12s.0d (£82.60p) in donations whereas the projected cost was £274.10s.0d.

The building of the school was by this time well under way. The site chosen was a plot of ground in part of Church Croft, "abutting upon the street lying opposite to Widow Harpur's Buildings and being in quantity about 12 yards frontage next to the street and thirteen yards deep." This describes the middle section of the older buildings now standing in Church Street (then Sidney Road).

The size of the schoolroom internally was twenty-nine feet long, eighteen feet wide, fifteen and a half feet to the ceiling of the rafters. "The new school, allowing an area of six square feet for each child will accommodate fifty to sixty children in one room to be Sunday and daily school."

On April 9th 1845 however the Rev. Howard wrote again to the National Society asking for more time to repay the £40 grant. "The school is roofed in but it is found impossible to complete it within the period of the Society's grant."

A Trust Deed for the land was signed and sealed on May 20th 1845; it set out the aspirations for the school subjects in reading, writing, arithmetic, geography, scripture, history and for the girls, needlework. The main witness to the document was the Bishop of Lichfield and it was dictated by the Reverend Frederick Emanuel Curzon, vicar of Mickleover and Littleover. He was a rather colourful character being expelled from Oxford and Cambridge Universities, his father purchasing his MA and his mother paying his subsequent gambling debts. The management and control was in the names of the Rev. Henry Reginald Chandos Pole, Rector of Radbourne, the Rev. John Garton Howard, vicar of St. Michael's, Derby, Edward Sacheveral Chandos Pole of Radbourne and William Williamson of Littleover.

The two centre windows of the present school building in Church Street are in the earliest schoolrooms built in 1845.

To raise the money outstanding from the original costings a "Bazaar for the sale of useful and fancy articles in aid of Littleover National School" was advertised in the *Derby Mercury* issue of August 27th 1845. The dates set for the event were September 17th and 18th with a charge of sixpence for admission; local ladies were willing to act as patrons. Among them was Lady Blane, wife of Sir Hugh Seymour Blane who was renting the Victorian mansion, "The Pastures" on Rykneld Road. Today it survives as a hospital. Sir Hugh Blane's father, Sir Gilbert, was instrumental in introducing lime juice for British sailors after discovering that the lack of vitamin C was causing scurvy in the Navy. Sir Hugh was a Lieutenant Colonel in the army and it is thought he fought at the Battle of Waterloo.

The advertisement for the Bazaar described a shortfall of £70, the sum needed to complete the building of the new school. It also stated that the grants from the societies would not be forthcoming unless the amount was reached. Donations had been promised which included £20 each from the Rev. Curzon, the Rev. Howard and Chandos Pole. Her Majesty the Queen Dowager had also donated £10.

A paragraph in the *Derby Mercury* of September 3rd explains the supply of items for the bazaar had proved to be considerable and extra money had been added by a subscription from Sir Hugh Blane and a friend of his from Quarndon.

In the week following the proposed dates of the sale a further notice appeared in the *Mercury* on September 24th stating that due to bad weather a large quantity of the items for sale had remained undisposed. Derby Solicitor and Littleover resident, William Williamson, offered his house as the venue for a further bazaar to be held "with the stalls full of fancy work". The advert also announced that £42.17s.6¹/₂d (£42.88p) had been raised at the first sale. The committee succeeded in raising all the money required plus a surplus. The final documentary evidence on the founding of the school is dated October 3rd 1845 certifying the completion of the school initially known as Littleover National School and later St. Peter's Church of England School. All the legal niceties were tied up with the signing of the deed by the Trustees

August advertisement in Derby Mercury

September 24th advertisement.

The rear of the Diocesan Training College built in 1815 in Uttoxeter Road, Derby.

and enrolled at the Chancery on August 22nd with a draft of the Trust Deed submitted to the National Society.

The building consisted of two classrooms with a partition between. In addition a cottage was provided for the schoolmaster and mistress with a joint salary of £28.4.0d (£28.20p). The 1846 *Bagshaws Directory of Derbyshire* also names the master as Thomas Manifold, aged 40. He took charge of forty-five boys and twenty girls. The parents of the sixty-five children had to pay fees.

The position and status of teachers was rated very low. This was highlighted in an inspector's report for Derbyshire in 1841. "Not one in three had ever attended even for a few weeks any kind of training school whatsoever, and this small proportion must be rated lower still if the inquiry were to be made as to those who had profited by such attendance." The only recruits for extra staff in the first twenty-five years of the school's life were pupil-teachers.

To improve the teaching skills and create the staff for a growing number of Church of England schools the Bishop of Lichfield, John Lonsdale, initiated the building of a college for training female teachers. This became the Diocesan Training College, the first institution for higher education in Derby.

Part of the completed building of 1851 still stands in Uttoxeter New Road, Derby.

In the 1838 fourth annual report on the Poor Law Committee Dr Kay stated that, "certain of the most intelligent scholars" were selected to be trained to the occupation of teachers; and in 1846 the Committee of Council for Education brought into execution the Apprenticeship of pupil-teachers who were at least thirteen years of age and signed on for a five-year period.

The system was introduced into England from Holland but the plan of being bound as apprentices came to an end after the 1870 Education Act.

By the middle of the century State education was becoming necessary even though the Anglican Church had laid claim to the largest percentage of schools and the control of nearly all the training colleges. Governments were wary of increasing taxation or local rates to fund education or to impose universal, compulsory attendance. Charles Dickens *Dombey and Son* was published the year St. Peter's School opened and Mr. Dombey seemed to express the feelings of the majority. "I am far from being friendly to what is called by persons of levelling sentiments, general education. But it is necessary that the inferior classes should continue to be taught to know their position and to conduct themselves properly. So far, I approve of schools."

A system of "payment by results" was introduced in 1862 which had the effect of imposing a national curriculum defined by the Codes. Lists of subjects enabled schools to gain grant income when pupils passed the appropriate examination. Initially it discouraged wider education beyond the three Rs and led to mechanical systems of teaching but it focussed the teachers mind on "cash earning" subjects such as reading short passages from newspapers, writing from dictation and doing arithmetic. The Code did achieve an acceptable level of literacy shown by a sharp rise in elementary school attendance nationwide to over a million by 1866.

This was the year when Littleover became a parish in its own right, separating from Mickleover for the first time since Saxon times. Log Books and Admission Registers began and were maintained at St. Peter's School. Mr. Thomas Richards who was trained at Highbury was the teacher now and his early entries in 1866 tell of enrolling scholars in Binn's Admission Register; returning Government Papers and giving cautions to pupils for lateness.

On March 12th 1866 Mr. Richards received the School Inspector's

Report which was very critical. "The classes should improve in reference to their Knowledge: they are also deficient in Writing, Spelling and Arithmetic. The Reading in the lower part of the School is Very Fair. The master has scarcely been one Year in charge, and has not yet had time to effect any decided improvement."

The inspector did not accept the average attendance figure of 40 as stated in the Manager's Return and calculated that 36 was the correct figure. "The Grant under Article 40 (a) has therefore been calculated upon that number. My Lords hope that the inspector will be able to report great improvement in the Instruction next year."

He also reported that he did not agree with the desks being set against the wall. "Such an arrangement of the furniture has been found, by experience to be much less convenient than groups of parallel desks and benches." He enclosed a memorandum which he thought may have been useful to improve the situation. He goes on, "it is very desirable that steps should at once be taken to make an effectual separation between the boys and girls offices (lavatories) and to render the urinal more private." The next entry, March 14th is interesting in that there was no school on that day owing to a cattle plague.

The school was inspected for the Diocese on April 25th by the Reverend Fieldson who expressed himself highly pleased with the efficiency of the school and stating in his report that the reading was, "the best I ever heard in any school – especially the 3rd Class who are in every subject far above the average." Under the heading "Abstract" he makes special mention of Fannie Browne's work. In the Enrolment Register her father's occupation has been given as "Farmer" against the largest majority of other children's fathers being "Labourers". Fannie left school in 1866 to begin an apprenticeship with a milliner. She was given special mention in the remarks column as being "Regular, attentive and well conducted."

On May 1st there was only a small attendance of girls at school owing to the local custom of walking with flowers at the usual spring festival in the village. Many children were not at school for a week when hay harvesting commenced on June 24th. An annual event for the children was the Summer Tea Party given by local benefactor of the church and School Manager, Mr. J. T. Morley, in his garden at Fairfield House on the Derby to Burton road, close to what is now Warwick Avenue.

The average attendance in July was 44, rising to 62 on November 14th.

ENROLMENT.

NAME.	Date.	Age.		Residence.	Occupation of Parent. (Underline when not entitled to receive the Grant, Art. 4, R.C.)
		Y.	M.		
Browne Fannie	18 .			Littleover	Farmer
Brayfield Polly				—	Labourer
Oliver Maria				—	
Oliver Mary				—	Pointsman
Harfield Martha				—	(Father dead)
Holden Emily				—	Labourer
Oliver Lucy	62 . 10			—	
Vickers Sarah				—	
Hind Judith	61 / 11			—	
Bryan Mary	65 / 4			—	
Bird Agnes				—	
Brayfield Agnes	62 . 5			—	
Bryan Emma	62 : 10			—	
Holden M. A.				—	
Vickers Louisa	62 . 11	—		—	
Fountain Edith	62 . 8			—	
Hodgkinson Annie				—	
Longmore Martha				—	
Hind Eliza				—	
Pegg Rose Violet				—	
Harfield Eliza				—	
Usy Edward				—	Farmer
Oliver Isaac				—	Pointsman
Tatlow Hiram				—	Mechanic
Pass George				—	Labourer
Fountain William				—	—
Seals Henry	65 . 3			—	Gardener
Gibson Joseph				—	(Father dead)
Oliver George (W.)				—	Labourer
Hemingway Henry				—	Farmer
Wass Walter				—	Labourer
Musgrove Solomon				—	—
Ault Charles				—	—

The first sheet of St Peter's Church of England School Register in 1866.

Another week of absenteeism was in early October when the children were employed picking potatoes. The year ended with a note in the Log Book on, "the observance of punctuation stops." A vacation of eleven days for Christmas followed.

In 1867 the mood in society was changing and Matthew Arnold, one of the most energetic school inspectors at this time, observed in his Report to the Council of Education that, "throughout my district I find the idea of compulsory education becoming a familiar idea with those who are interested in schools."

In a *Journal of British Studies* in 1993, Jonathan Rose states that 66.2 per cent of children in this period enjoyed their schooling which goes against the usual impression that the working-class regarded education as something of a drudgery. As in all generations the minority broke the rules. On January 7th in the 1867 Log Book four boys had to be "severely corrected for unseemly conduct in the House of God on Sunday." In July, boys were cautioned about their anger at sports and two boys were punished for fighting during play hours.

Early in the year the inspector gave the teacher another critical report. "The Master, Mr. Richards, has entered my Report in the Log Book and signed it with his own name adding the word Secretary to it – this has been done twice and each time spelled Secretary – Secetary – he has also spelled deficient – defecient – and the word repetition, has been five times spelled repitition." The Inspector made other unfavourable comments about certain procedures not being carried out which led to a cut in grants. The main function of the Inspector was to "collect facts and information and report on them to the Government." What they found in those early days highlighted the teachers' lack of training. This was a period of payment by results and the code demanded that examination of pupils took place in schools and was conducted by the inspector.

"This test has not been satisfied by the examination of your school, and, therefore My Lords have ordered one-tenth to be deducted from the Grant under Article 52(a) for failure to exhibit a sufficient advanced instruction. Another tenth has been deducted from the Grant under same article on account of the defective instruction in Arithmetic", he concluded.

Later in the year, on the August 15th the installation of gas fittings began in school for the lighting. The work continued until October 3rd. In

November Mr. Richards reports of the severe cold in the classroom owing to the unavailability of a fire as the chimney needed repair. On the third day he says it was too cold to use either a pen or pencil so he was confined to giving oral lessons.

From a revised code in 1857 some clerics saw an opportunity for a good career through HMI. The Government Inspector is named as the Rev. J. J. Blandford in the 1868 Log Book and, although the report this year is a little better, the Grant is still reduced by one-tenth owing to very unsatisfactory results from the children's examination on Arithmetic. "The issue of Mr. Richard's Certificate must be defered for the present." He is still acting as a Probationer. The report also asks: "I am to inquire why the managers think it advisable that the teacher should not occupy the Residence which belongs to him officially."

It appears that Mr. Richards was not a popular appointment although the 1869 Report, signed by the Rev. William Buckwell, began encouragingly with good remarks about discipline, religious knowledge and reading. However no Grant was payable due to an article in the code of practice not being satisfactory. "Next year My Lord will require the Accounts to be audited by some other person than the Treasurer."

The question of the teacher's accommodation did not appear to have been settled. "I am to request an answer to the enquiry made last year why the master does not occupy the residence which belongs to him officially." However Mr. Richards does receive his Certificate.

The entries in the Log Book continue in March and April 1869 on the same theme, most lessons going through the motions of reading and writing, but concentrating mainly on religious teaching. Nothing is written about the outcome of the school house or whether Richards found better employment because of his Certificate, but on May 19th the Log Book states that a new teacher, Mr. John Hunt, took charge of the school. The following week the girls were being taught needlework by a new mistress, Mrs. Hunt. Again, there is no record of them taking the house provided.

Difficulties continued regarding attendance when two boys were required to leave school for "parent service". Entries of school equipment arriving is interesting: "$^1/_2$ ream ruled foolscap, 4 doz penholders, 1 gross of pens, 2 doz lead pencils, 2 sets reading sheets for lower classes." First and Second classes commenced writing on ruled paper on the same day.

Aids for the pupils were happening on a regular basis after Mr. Hunt's arrival. Twenty-five table cards (used for arithmetic) and one pint of ink paid for by the teacher was received from the printers, Bemrose. He also employed a Monitor, Louis Spencer, for the first time.

Typically, for this country, the weather changed dramatically in a matter of a week. On June 7th 1869, one boy, William Parker, had to be sent home on account of his nose bleeding due to the heat and two days later Rufus Spencer suffered the same fate along with another boy Henry Hague.

At school assembly Mr. Hunt gave a talk on the importance of good manners and behaviour when spoken to by visitors. Discipline was an important part of the teacher's duties. When he detected the stealing of school articles on the June 15th he punished the offenders and separated them from their classes; he thought Louisa Vickers was the ringleader. His punishment sometimes brought complaints from the parents. John Parker was punished for fighting in school and kept in for one hour. "His mother came at 5 o'clock and disapproved of the punishment", the Log Book records. The mother of Louis Spencer, the boy used as a Monitor, suggested an alternative way of dealing with her son. Mr. Hunt had given him three "stripes" across the desk for obstinate disobedience. He then made him stand on a form to shame him but Mrs. Spencer suggested that home lessons should have been given. He also had to deal with a complaint from Mr. Sow about seven boys shouting on his premises.

School fees were a cause for complaint from some parents. John Parker brought a message from his parents who were unhappy about paying 6d (3p) per week for their two children, John and William. They sent 3d (1p) for each boy. Mr. Hunt explained to the boys that their parents had agreed to the charge and by the afternoon a further 6d was brought to the school by John. Mrs. Oliver called one evening to say she could not pay 6d a week for her son George who was over fourteen years of age and 6d was returned. George had been re-admitted two months earlier and had been given private lessons.

Parents were not afraid to offer opinions. Mrs. Holden, a parent of four children disapproved of the school closing for a week in September for harvest. In fact, she complained about "any holidays at all". Mrs. Hague from Sinfin however called to express satisfaction of the teaching received by her daughter, Mary. One objection from parents was about the sweeping of the school by the children. This was resolved by a person being employed to carry out the duty.

The patrons of St. Peter's regularly displayed their public service. John Tempest Morley (School Manager) annually arranged the children's summer treat at his home. He also regularly visited the school to examine the children's writing. Lady Blane from Pastures House offered patchwork for the needlework class, supplying cotton for the girls. She often sent her maid to inspect the work. Lady Blane also sent a message to say that the school fee of 2d (1p) for Thomas Vickers should be paid quarterly.

Music was a big part of school life which included a choir. A half holiday was given on June 23rd for the choir to attend the annual Choir Festival at St. Andrew's Church, Derby. The school harmonium was obviously in constant use for it had to be sent for repair but was returned within a week, in November. In the winter of 1869 lessons in English history are first recorded at the school; the subject being on the Saxon line of kings. Gas lighting was becoming beneficial and used on a regular basis on the premises it "being too dark for lessons without."

English society was changing throughout the 1860s with numerous attempts in Parliament to make elementary education available to all but how it should be provided was always controversial. The Trade Union Congress had their opinions. The craft unions they represented were becoming more organised due to the number of white collar workers doubling in the 1860s thus keeping pace with the needs of the industrial economy.

The Liberals had formed a new Government in 1870 and grasped the nettle by introducing England's Elementary Education Bill led by William Edward Forster. Forster's father was a Quaker preacher who became a leader in the fight to abolish slavery. William married a non Quaker, Jane Arnold, the sister of Matthew, and accepted the penalty of being expelled from the Society of Friends. William Edward Forster was elected MP for Bradford in 1861 and appointed by Gladstone as the Vice-President of the Committee of Council on Education. He later relied on his brother-in-law's vast knowledge of Education in England as an inspector.

The Bill which Forster presented to Parliament was enacted but not without numerous amendments; chiefly the dropping of the compulsory education clause. The churches argued that state schools would be godless while the Nonconformists feared Anglican dominance. The religious issue remained a serious problem but the Bill provided for the establishment of local school boards with authority to raise funds for elementary schools and to charge fees to parents. Other aspects came to the fore with industrialists raising serious questions. In the Great Exhibition in 1851 British manufacturers won most of the orders. When industrialists displayed their wares at the International Exposition in Paris in 1867, they won only ten of the ninety classes. The Royal Society of Arts reported "the general deficiency of the technical knowledge of our best workmen."

Various inquiries were set up, one headed by the Duke of Devonshire in 1875 which turned out to be critical of most grammar schools for refusing to reform the curriculum to allow more hours for science. This of course was all aimed at the middle classes and private and proprietary schools which were patronised by business. Nevertheless it was a change in outlook and one that would eventually affect future generations.

When Forster introduced the Bill to the House of Commons he declared: "Our aim, then, must be (1) to cover the country with good schools, and (2) to get the parents to send their children to those schools."

At least the 1870 Education Act began to make a positive move in improving the schooling for the children of the poor. Inevitably there were gaps needed to be filled such as ending the "payment by results" system and increasing the number of teachers which the new changes would demand.

Local school boards were set-up to provide "Board Schools" which gave non-denominational teaching. Church schools were termed voluntary schools which gave instructional and religious teaching. St. Peter's Log Books for the next few years after 1870 show no dramatic changes to the curriculum. This is not surprising as it was never Forster's intention to destroy the existing position of schools but to fill the gaps left by the voluntary group. If the quality of education was found to be "sufficient, efficient and suitable" the Bill would leave it in place. The responsibility therefore was left to the School Managers and in the case of St. Peter's School, the Church.

The Inspector's Report in February 1870 was favourable apart from Arithmetic which it was hoped would improve although this would not concern Mr. and Mrs. Hunt as their position as master and mistress of the school for the previous ten months came to an end. Mr. and Mrs. Benjamin Toft were appointed and began their duties on Monday March 7th. Mr. Toft's first duties involved having to caution boys about damaging a wall adjoining the school premises and others breaking school windows. A few boys out of the 1st Class attended an examination on Scripture and Liturgy at Langley in April and on June 23rd there was no school as the master accompanied the choir to the Melbourne Choir Festival.

The challenge for improvement was taken up at the end of the 1870 when the Rev. Buckwell called at the school on November 16th to show the plan of a proposed enlargement of the schoolroom at an estimated cost of £120.

In March 1871, the year following the Education Act, ten out of fourteen schools recorded had either discontinued or their fees were too high to come under the requirements of the Act. When investigations were made many of these were being conducted in ill-ventilated rooms, overcrowded and classed as "inefficient".

Work began on extending the school by sixteen feet on February 23rd 1871 by knocking through the east wall at an estimated cost of £120. Teaching took place in the reading-room. Four days later an application was made to the National Society for a grant of £45. Local funds had already raised £45 and a further £30 had been promised.

The Committee of Council on Education sent a document containing the rules which were to be observed in planning and fitting schools. St. Peter's was now to becoming termed a "mixed" school with classrooms laid out according to the regulations. Each class required a separate teacher, even though it may only be a monitor acting for the hour. The rules state, "without such provision it is impossible to keep all the children in a school actively employed at the same time." Where apprenticed pupil-teachers were used as assistants, at public expense, it became important to furnish them with all the necessary material. The master was instructed to leave himself time to observe the manner in which his assistants or monitors taught and watch the collective working of his school. The inspector ignored the rules that wood partitions or diamond paned windows were not allowed. Both were inserted in the original building in 1845.

The Committee of Council's instructions on the situation of desks and benches was very detailed. They stated that they were not to be fixed firmly to the floor, "but not so as to be easily pushed out of place by accident."

COMMITTEE OF COUNCIL ON EDUCATION.

R U L E S

TO BE OBSERVED IN

PLANNING AND FITTING UP SCHOOLS.

By Authority of the Committee of Council on Education.

LONDON:

PRINTED BY GEORGE EDWARD EYRE AND WILLIAM SPOTTISWOODE,
PRINTERS TO THE QUEEN'S MOST EXCELLENT MAJESTY.

FOR HER MAJESTY'S STATIONERY OFFICE.

27514.

1871.

The 1871 rules sent to St Peter's Church School for the extension to the school.

The desks should also be either quite flat or very slightly inclined. "The objections to the inclined desk are, that pencils, pens, &c. are constantly slipping from it, and that it cannot be conveniently used as a table." There were also objections to the flat desk as it made the children stoop. "A raised ledge in front of a desk interferes with the arm in writing." St. Peter's records don't tell us which type of desk was chosen but the photograph taken in 1913 on page 54, shows them to be flat with no raised ledge. Teaching commenced in the new classroom on 17th April.

Central Government's radical ideas were not always trusted. A new revised education code of regulations was issued by the Education Department only a year after the introduction of the Act . This offered a grant of three shillings a head for a pass in not more than two specific subjects.

Locally a meeting was held in St. Werburgh's schoolroom, in Curzon Street, Derby. The Chairman, the Rev. Wilkinson, opened the proceedings by stating that in his view the new revised code offered more advantages to managers and teachers of schools. However, to howls of laughter, he said they could not expect too much from the Chancellor of the Exchequer.

The furthest gable on the present school is the 1871 schoolroom.

A concession in the new code was in favour of night schools where scholars could be taught by a pupil-teacher who had served his apprenticeship.

Overall the meeting was of the opinion that "the new code would prove beneficial to elementary education, but it is capable of modification in many of its details." Mr. Bland from Duffield supported the resolution but was critical that no encouragement had been made to the masters for the additional time and labour they would have to expend in order to qualify their scholars for the attainment of the capitation grant. "Hear, hear" was heard throughout the hall. The resolution was carried.

The same response was made when Mr. White complained that conditions set out to obtain grants in night schools were too stringent. He thought the second resolution at the meeting should consider that sixty opening a year with an average of thirty attendances would be sufficient for the Government grant and the age limit set at eighteen should be increased to twenty-one. This was carried unanimously.

A third resolution was proposed, "that this meeting is of the opinion that no reduction should be made in the existing Government grant to voluntary schools. The proposer of the resolution, Mr. Cummings, thought the object of the Government was clearly to drive the voluntary schools down and to promote the School Boards. He distrusted the minute of the Education Council. A further resolution that the standard of girls be lowered as they expended much time on sewing was carried amidst the applause of the women in the audience. The meetings ended with all the resolutions being embodied in the form of a petition and forwarded to the House of Commons.

Attendance at St. Peter's was low throughout the summer months of 1871 which led to the closure on odd days. One was in celebration of the church being re-opened after considerable improvements. A few children were absent in the first week of October picking blackberries and potatoes. The year ended on a positive note with the installation of a new stove.

In May 1872 the School Manager, Mr. Morley, died. Later two large stained-glass windows in the parish church were dedicated to him by his wife and the congregation. The annual treat for the children was now held in the Vicarage grounds in Shepherds Lane (now Normanton Lane).

In 1873 Parliament passed an Act which imposed compulsory attendance on those parents who were receiving Poor Law Relief. Forster at that time could not get the full agreement to general compulsion of attendance which he would have wished.

Eighty-seven children (49 boys, 38 girls) were present when the school was examined in February of that year by the Rev. Blandford; an increase of twenty-five from November 1866. Forty-one pupils were presented for examination on several subjects from six classes. Five took the extra subjects of Poetry and Grammar. Prizes were awarded to twelve girls for Sewing; one of them Sarah Gilman, who became a pupil-teacher three years later. The prizes were given by Lady Blane, Mrs. Hurst and Mrs. Buckwell, the wife of the school inspector.

Intakes had risen to 102 (59 boys, 43 girls) in February 1874 and fees were raised in the higher part of the school.

Another favourable inspector's report was received on March 12th but, "a classroom is much needed on account of the number of little children."

General examinations took place in the school in October 1875.

Presented in	How many	No of Passes in				
		R.	W.	A.	G.	P.
Standard I	18	14	15	13		
" II	7	7	7	5		
" III	9	9	7	6		
" IV	1	1	1	1	1	1
" V	4	4	3	2	3	3
" VI	2	2	2	2	2	2
Totals	41	37	35	29	6	6

Sample of tests in arithmetic:
Standard III

$£22.10s.8\frac{1}{2}d \times 128$

$£90.13s.8\frac{3}{4}d \div 7$

Reduce 320 guineas to halfpence.

What will lb tea cost if I give $£116.19s.0\frac{3}{4}$ for 225lbs.

(Answers at the end of this chapter).

Work was set in motion to convert a cottage for the purpose in June and was completed on 3rd July. It was recommended that the school obtain the services of a transfer pupil-teacher. On August 3rd the newly-appointed assistant mistress, Frances North, began her duties. Mr. Toft was due to receive his teacher's certificate.

Attendances fluctuated for the first five years of the Education Act even after the employment of children under eight was forbidden in the 1873 Agricultural Children's Act. It must be stressed that most laws regulating the employment of children were evaded. St. Peter's reports that some boys were absent in 1875 as they were needed "to get up potatoes", although it does not state their age. Ada Vickers, aged eight and a half, had returned to school after being kept at home a long time for "usefulness". She had been admitted to school five years earlier.

In March 1875 Mr. J. Noble called to bring the children's attention to a complaint of the damage being done to the insulators of telegraph poles by stone throwing. He had taken over the role as School Manager and was responsible for the children's well-being. Following the rules set out by the Committee of Council on Education in 1871 Mr. Noble had overseen the laying of the school playground in May and it was opened to the children after a few remarks by the Vicar.

An Act in 1876 brought in compulsory schooling in the form of a bye-law. Some progressive School Boards or Attendance Committees took up the option, but this only covered half the elementary school population. Even then evasion of the laws was widespread. At Littleover Sarah Jane Dakin's father, from Mickleover, was summoned by the School Board to explain the irregular attendance of his child.

The 1870 Education Act demanded more teachers but this proved to be impossible. Inspectors were granting Certificates to teachers and assistant teachers who had not undergone either training or examination; even pass standards in training colleges were being lowered. Due to the overwhelming demand for places The Training College could admit only half of the pupil-teachers who qualified for entry. This led to a decrease in certificated teachers in the first ten years of the Act. At St. Peter's two pupil-teachers commenced their duties in summer 1876; Sarah Gilman in August, followed by Mary Toft, daughter of the master.

The spread of diseases was a constant threat to school attendance. In October measles hit the village leaving only forty-seven children in school. This fell to thirty-seven on November 3rd with only two all week in Standard III. Harriet Musgrove, an infant, is the only child reported as dying but a fortnight later there were only fifty-nine children at school, Littleover suffering a bout of 'Scarletina" (Scarlet Fever).

The two pupil-teachers were examined on Saturday January 20th 1877 in Holy Trinity School, Derby. Sarah Gilman was found to be fit and healthy enough for her office as teacher and her conduct perfectly satisfactory along with her punctuality and obedience. Mary Annie Toft, the daughter of the master and mistress was expected to progress owing to her own efforts and the example of her parents. A Government Report stated that Sarah Gilman "has passed fairly under Article 19(c) but should attend to Composition."

In March 1878 the children were allowed a few minutes play on fine mornings. Attendance was improving slowly with only fourteen short of a full school of seventy-five. The usual half-day holidays were allowed including Festival Day at Derby Arboretum on 1st July.

The same names of staff are recorded in the Log Book for March 1879 with a principal teacher, Benjamin Toft and two pupil-teachers, Sarah Gilman and Mary Toft. There was concern about one of them, Mary, who would not be recognised until her indentures had been completed and a suitable salary paid.

For the last two or three years discussions had taken place about compulsory attendance. Section 4 of the Education Act of 1876 set up bye-laws which made it the statutory duty of parents to ensure their children received elementary instruction in reading, writing and arithmetic. The Act also provided that no child under ten should be employed, nor any child between ten and fourteen unless they had either (a) passed a Standard IV examination in the three Rs and been given a "Labour Certificate" by HMI, or (b) made up to 250 attendances during each of five years, at not more than two schools (this became known as the "Dunce's Certificate"). The Act was left to local authorities to establish provisions which could either be School Boards where they existed, or School Attendance Committees. Although additional bye-laws were produced there still appeared to be widespread evasion of the laws. Employers were as reluctant as ever to relinquish the cheap labour of children as were the parents who, sadly, were so reliant on the money the children brought into the home. By 1880 A. J. Mundella, Vice-President of the Committee of Council, (E. M. Forster was now the Secretary for Ireland in Gladstone's cabinet), introduced a new Act enforcing compulsion. This required all School Boards and Attendance Committees which had not already passed bye-laws to do so forthwith. Once more this compulsion was within narrow limits, with its universal application being the only improvement on 1876. Children continued to abscond over the ensuing years mainly due to the lack of imaginative instruction in some schools and harsh discipline, including corporal punishment.

In 1880 Voluntary Schools (which included St. Peter's), were teaching over seventy per cent of children who were entitled to elementary education in their catchment areas but their revenue did not come from the local rates as in the case of the Board Schools. They had three main sources of income:

Reproduced with the permission of Derby Local Studies Library

1883 Ordnance Survey Map which shows the school plan with the 1871 expansion from the first school built in 1845.

Government grants; pupil fees and voluntary contributions from private individuals or collections in the church. The first two raised similar amounts in St. Peter's accounts of 1880; a £55.14s.0d (£55.70p) grant and £53.14s.6d (£53. 73p) from fees. A further £2 was raised by the hire of the schoolroom. The grant figures make interesting comparisons with 3/- (15p) for the general subjects, 4/- (20p) for specific subjects and a weighty 8/- (40p) for infants who qualified. All these were paid only on an average attendance throughout the year. Mr. Toft, the principal teacher, was paid £107.12s.0d (£107.60p) in 1880, (this could include Mrs. Toft's salary as sewing mistress). Two pupil-teachers shared £28.15s.0d (£28.75p) with Sarah Gilman, now in her fourth year apprenticeship, earning a little more than Mary Toft who was in her third year.

In March 1881 Sarah Gilman's duties as a principal teacher came to an end as she had completed her apprenticeship. Nothing is noted about her future career but she continued to visit the school from time to time. She was one of thousands of children aged between thirteen and eighteen who played a large part in the running of schools in the first decade after the 1870 Education Act.

New schools around Littleover were beginning to open; Normanton in 1880 and Mickleover Board School 1881. These began to take pupils away from St. Peter's. William Thomas and Joseph Blood came for just a week in 1882 and then returned to the school at Mickleover. However this did not seem to affect the full intake of pupils in 1882 as the highest average attendance of 119.5 was recorded on 1st May. The school had to close for three weeks in the following month due to a further outbreak of measles. Although there is no record of child deaths it was thought by the School Managers to be a safe decision under the circumstances. Measles continued to affect the level of attendance throughout the next few years.

Early Education standards continued along similar lines in 1883. The school admitted Henry Stoppard, "a big boy." They tested him in Standard I subjects but he failed in all; this failure was highlighted by his spelling "dond" for down and "fas" for fire for example. Henry was nearly ten years old and his father, Aaron, was a coachman. He stayed for only eleven months due to the family leaving the village.

The Government Report was becoming repetitive. "Discipline and Order good. The standard work and Geography were well done. Grammar very fair." Mary Toft was now mentioned in the Log Book as an assistant mistress on the school staff. Earlier however she could not be admitted to the examination for certificates, "until My Lords have received a Report on her Needlework from HMI. Article 57(b)2. Code of 1882." The Elementary School Code of that year had made various changes which included a seventh grade and scholarships to endowed grammar schools were created for promising children.

In November 1883 Mary Toft was away all week undergoing examination at Derby Training College for a Teacher's Certificate. She took second year's papers and a monitor was employed during her absence. Although this was the first mention in the Log Book of the Training College being used by the school, such part-time study was not a very satisfactory answer to the training of teachers.

Familiar objections to the original "gaps" in the Education Act were still being discussed by Parliament. Answers needed to be found for abolishing "payment by results" and provision for the training of teachers and inspectors. The Royal Commission on Technical Education of 1882 had confirmed that England's industrial superiority was being overtaken by Prussia, France and the United States. The Paris Exposition had certainly driven the point home so the Commission's recommendation was to introduce technical and scientific education into the secondary schools. Admittedly a dozen or so civic universities were founded in the last quarter of the century but these were all created and funded by local industrialists.

Due to pressure from the white-collar class the Franchise Act or Third Parliamentary Reform Act gave the vote to almost all adult males. This included the agricultural workers in Littleover and the huge army of mine workers. Domestic servants, bachelors living with their parents and those of no fixed address were not included; even so the Act added two million votes in the country.

One of the other big concerns not tackled by the 1870 Act was the health and well-being of the nation's children. The medical forum the *Lancet* said in 1884 that the system of education was, "demonstrating that they were underfed."

The Vice-President of the Committee of Council at the time, A. J. Mundella saw no reason to change things; rather to promote a voluntary system. He became the president of The Central Council for Promoting

Self-Supporting Penny Dinners but it was not a surprise to many that this did not work.

No mention of dinners is made in St. Peter's School 1884 Log Book but in his report early in the year the inspector shows particular concern for the infants' health. "The children under seven have been pretty fairly taught, but the classroom in which they are instructed is dark and narrow and wholly unsuitable. Unless proper accommodation is provided I shall have great hesitation in recommending a Grant another year."

Five new desks arrived earlier in the year and plans were put forward to enlarge the 1845 section of the building westwards. From August 11th the school was closed for six weeks for the work to take place. Although the school re-opened on September 22nd the workmen were still busy in the largest room. They interrupted classes for a further month before work commenced "colouring" (painting) the whole school. After completion of the new classroom it was used for the first time on November 3rd. Men were then employed levelling land for the playground.

Alice Timms completed here apprenticeship as a pupil-teacher at the beginning of 1885 when there was a fall in attendance due to another outbreak of measles. The

The 1884 school building extension at the west end of the present school.

inspector makes comment about the new classroom. "The school buildings have been enlarged and otherwise greatly improved. The principal room in one part is rather dark." To solve the problem two sky-lights were inserted in the roof in August.

Britains position as the greatest workshop of the world had been diminishing for a number of years. Since the end of the American Civil War in 1865 the United States had progressed rapidly, particularly in the production of wheat which had flooded free-trade England and brought about a great agricultural depression in 1886. Those in high places laid the blame at the door of technical education. There was no evidence of this but it was another turning point in Government investigations into education.

Government grants were still somewhat dependent on attendance figures in 1886 but there appears to have been no significant decrease in funds at St. Peter's with 145 pupils present when the school was inspected.

Another routine HMI's report on the curriculum was received although there was some hesitation in recommending a Good Merit Grant for older children. The younger daughter of Mr. and Mrs. Toft, Edith had passed her fourth year examination as a pupil-teacher but, "she must not be allowed to serve in school for a greater number of hours than is allowed by paragraph I of her Memorandum of Agreement." Her sister Mary took the Certificate Examination in November.

The school staff in 1887 consisted entirely of the Toft family. Benjamin, principle teacher (1st Class), Mary A. Toft, assistant teacher and Edith M. Toft who had now attained the necessary qualifications to become an assistant teacher. Three of their sons attended the school. Hubert Harry started in April 1887 aged six years and eleven months; Leonard in February 1889 aged seven and Frederick was aged eight years and four months when he started in July 1893.

This years inspector's report made note that "the wall forming one of the sides of the room is very damp and should at once be attended to." The dampness was rectified, the ceiling repaired and other repairs were undertaken in the building in early June. The school broke up for a week's holiday as the classrooms were required for Queen Victoria's Jubilee.

Children were absent with infectious diseases during the year: whooping cough in July and measles in December when the school had to be closed. The managers took the opportunity to have the classrooms whitewashed, painted and cleaned during this period.

The Local Government Act of 1888 set up elected County Councils to replace the Justices of the Peace who had administered county business since Tudor times.

While this Bill was being put through Parliament the Cross Commission under Lord Cross was formed to inquire into the working of the Elementary Education Acts in England and Wales. Its business was to research into how

The oldest parts of the school complex are in Church Street. The original 1845 schoolrooms are in the two centre windows, without the gables. The 1871 extension is on the far right and the final building in 1884 is on the left.

well the voluntary schools were performing under previous Acts. One chief inspector reported that it was doubtful whether it would be good to give a talented working class boy a scholarship to the university and thereby "lift him out of his own social station, and put him in one which is not congenial to him." The training of inspectors had been talked about for years as their tasks were becoming repetitious and people of quality were not being attracted to the post.

The Committee on the Commission issued both majority and minority views in their reports. The majority, which included Catholic Cardinal Manning and Anglican Bishop Temple, felt that school buildings were adequately supplied, the inspectorate good, the pupil-teacher system adequate and compulsory education to age eleven was sufficient. Their main complaint was the lack of finance in church-run schools. The minority view urged the abolition of the pupil-teacher system and wanted to adopt teachers' colleges which the Scotland system had chosen. This would provide the teachers with the necessary training after they had completed secondary school. Both factions however agreed on the need to abolish "payment-by-results." The Cross Commission's recommendation did lead to universities and university colleges establishing day training colleges to train teachers for public elementary schools. This helped solve the problem the Board Schools were facing as three-quarters of trained teachers were coming from denominational colleges, although large numbers were taking posts in Board Schools as the pay and working conditions were better.

Other different forms of rewards were given to schools after the Cross Commission and inspectors were freed of some of the drudgery.

The year of 1888 was a very eventful one for the nation. The Miners' Federation of Great Britain was founded, a landmark in the development of trade-unionism and the English Football League was formed. This was also the grim year of the multiple murders by "Jack the Ripper", who was never identified. Sadly for the world of schools and education, Matthew Arnold died suddenly in Liverpool on the April 15th. He was the energetic school inspector in the 1860s who had campaigned for a widening of the school curriculum. He was a poet of some note, whose famous work, *Dover Beach* was published in 1867.

St. Peter's School was inspected by Mr. J. W. Brigg. His report in 1869, although rather brief, showed concern for the weak written grammar of the girls in the upper standards who "did not answer satisfactorily in geography."

In another memorable year of change in the education of children, 1890, the school was thoroughly cleaned, colour washed and painted inside and out. A new door was also put up at the entrance to the boys' "offices" (lavatories). In higher places more recommendations of the Cross Commission were put into practice in the Code of Regulations for Public Elementary Schools. Better co-operation was being formed with the Education Department, who now recognised the teachers' professional associations. More importantly the end was in sight of the much hated payment by results system. A fixed grant of ten shillings per head, based on the examination of a sample of the pupils, was introduced but this too was discarded in the next few years. It was now the duty of the State to care for the physical welfare of the children which included sports and games plus the encouragement of teaching outdoors when applicable.

The new scale of fees commenced at Littleover Church School in September 1891 and in the following year there was a change of emphasis in the inspector's report. Suggestions for helping the infants by having a gallery of pictures of common animals was part of his remit. In cleanliness he thought a urinal was required for the infant boys. Following the Cross Commission it was now thought that the inspectors could help, not as critics, but as advisers to aid the performance of an important public work.

The fee grant for 1891 was reduced by £2.6s.9d (£2.34p) under the Elementary Education Act. This was due to the excess of fees received during the months of the previous October, November, December and January. The inspector was now allowed to visit without notice and Mr. Meggs carried out a short inspection on October 31st 1892. His brief notes mention the admission book being incomplete; that a thermometer was needed; concern over the short pencils; disinfectants should be used in the offices and there was still a need for a small urinal for the infant boys. The maintenance costs for the school included repairs to the skylights and water pipes and a rail-fence which had erected up on the road side of the playground for the children's safety.

The Government Report for 1893 thought the girls "ought not to be wholly ignorant of geography. . . . . More fixing should be done by them in their garments. . . . . Discipline is much too lax." He requested that a wood and glass partition "should be thrown across the room." This was completed during the Whitsuntide holiday.

All the village children had a treat in honour of the Royal Wedding when Prince George of Wales married Princess Mary of Teck. A fortnight later there was a low attendance on the afternoon of July 19th owing to a number of children having joined the Baptist Band of Hope. There was a school excursion to Locko Park at Spondon.

Further recommendations were made by the inspector, Mr. Meggs, when he visited in December. He thought the classrooms needed more light as the gas mantels were burning at 3.00pm. "It is desirable to replace the present diamond panes with plain glass." The windows should not all be closed either and cloakroom accommodation for boys was requested. In the same month assistant teacher in charge of Standards I and II, Edith Toft, attended a Certificate Examination.

Various bodies, one of which was the newly formed Independent Labour Party, were pressing for legislation which would enable county councils to administer secondary education. In 1894 a Royal Commission was appointed to consider the matter. Within a short space of time the Commissioners produced a report which turned out to be another big step in English educational history. Its principal aim was to form a central authority for secondary education under a new department headed by a Minister of Education and establish local authorities to oversee the second strand with wide powers to "supply, maintain, and aid schools" out of county rates. The machinery of Government as usual needed time to move things along. The same could be said of the School Managers at St. Peter's when reading the inspector's report of March 1894. He still complains about the lighting which was duly improved during the Easter holidays when the diamond panes were replaced with large squares.

In October only sixty seven pupils were present owing to another outbreak of measles in the village. The Vicar, Chairman of the School Managers, advised the closing of the school. It re-opened three and a half weeks later.

The inspectors report in March 1895 showed a marked improvement, particularly in English and Geography. "Considering the state of the master's health and the outbreak of measles during October the results deserve credit." Edith Toft's Certificate was forwarded to his office for endorsement.

Mr. Brigg, HM Sub Inspector of Schools visited on 17th October and suggested blinds and curtains be put up. The timetable should also allow for recreation at each opening of the school. He does not agree with one class of infants being taken into the main room during a needlework lesson, evidently only to be kept quiet. Seven of them are placed on a high form and six on three chairs (two on each) without anything to do.

Fifty years had now passed since St. Peter's School was founded and although progress had been made, there was still work to be done to improve education throughout the country. The recommendations from the Royal Commission in 1894 were still to come into being and there was also a need for an entirely new financial structure. There is no denying that literacy had improved enormously over the last fifty years. The supply of literate male workers had increased even faster than the demand for them in the 1890s. State subsidies rose sharply to offset the declining contribution of fees. Much of it went to reduce pupil-teacher ratios and an increase in the wages of teachers which improved teaching effectiveness.

Although a school leaver fifty years earlier was only ten years of age he mostly went straight into employment as a child labourer and did not need to be literate. By 1895 he could have applied for a job with better pay, keeping accounts, reading and writing instructions and reports or delivering telegrams which relied on the messenger being able to read the addresses on envelopes.

From 1895 onwards attempts were made to improve all aspects of school life, unfortunately World Wars and economic depressions did at times make things rather difficult. In only seven years, 1902, the second Education Act was passed by the House of Commons and the next chapter deals with its impact. The school at Littleover was to see the arrival of a new headmaster early in the century. His appointment proved to be an inspiration for the development of the school.

Answers to general examination on page 19. (1) £2,884 10s 8d; (2) £12 19s 1¼; (3) 161,280 influence: (4) 10s 4 ¼d.

CHAPTER TWO

A NEW HEADMASTER FIGHTS FOR CHANGE

1896 - 1917

The second fifty years of child education at St. Peter's Church School, Littleover, began with many improvements still being required, particularly in welfare. There was also further need for the tightening up of agreements. During these years a number of new Parliamentary Acts were implemented each having some effect on education in general and on St. Peter's in particular.

In 1896, the year the infant room in the school was enlarged, the country celebrated Queen Victoria's Diamond Jubilee and Britain reached the peak of its imperialistic ambitions.

Under the provisions of the Local Government Act of 1894 a meeting of the Parochial Electors of the Parish of Littleover was held at the schoolroom on Monday, March 9th 1896. Eleven men put their names forward to serve as Parish Councillors for the ensuing year. St. Peter's head teacher, Benjamin Toft was one of them but could only acquire enough votes to reach ninth position. Only six candidates could serve as Councillors.

New desks arrived for the infants' room at the beginning of 1897. After HMI's visit he reported that he was fairly pleased with the progress of the lower classes but he pointed out that as the class numbers now exceeded fifty a certificated teacher was required. In the mixed school attention was needed in the "object lessons"; however, after much hesitation, he recommended the higher grants.

For the first time a mid-week outing for the Sunday School scholars was arranged in July. They all travelled to Tutbury in wagons pulled by horses. Horses were still the main form of transport in the area at this time with buses being towed by the faithful beasts.

Mr. Toft had unsuccessfully been nominated to serve on Littleover Parish Council for the previous two elections but in 1898 only seven candidates stood for six seats. Benjamin Toft was successful on this occasion and one of the duties of the council in his first year was the appointment of J. G. Varty and Sons to catch moles in the parish at a salary of £4 per annum.

In July the school inspector insisted that a lavatory should be provided and by September one was installed in the boys' cloakroom.

1896.

Poetry for 1896-7. "The Chase" line 179 to 329. Lady of the Lake Std IV up; "The last Redoubt" Std IV. & "The Children's Hour" Stds I & II.
Geography IV upwards "Europe".

Object Lessons for Stds I, II & III.
Horse; Camel; Lion; Elephant;
Sheep; Hen; Goose; Sparrow; Ostrich;
Frog; Whale; Sugar; Iron;
Coal; Salt; Uses of Water; Glass;
Cotton; Linen; Silk; Leather; Tea;
Wheat; Barley; Potato Rain & Clouds;
Ice; Honesty; Industry; Obedience.

Object Lessons for Infants.
Horse b; Reindeer; Camel; Sheep b
Cow b; Lion; Cat; Dog;
A Ship; A Slate b; A Brick; An Orange
An egg b; Tea; Coffee; Oak Tree
Railway Station; Tram-cart; Coal; Wood
Wool; Industry; Obedience; Benevolence
The Baker b; Blacksmith b; Bricklayer; The Farm
Flowers & Fruits b; Form & Colour.

Approved,
W. T. Meggy.

Object lessons of 1896 for the mixed and infants school.

In the 1890s post-elementary education was in a confused and some said illegal state. The 1870 Act had not included a formal leaving age and the children who passed through seven standards usually left school at the age of ten. Only about half of them reached Standard VII but some wanted to stay on to further their education. They were catered for in extra classrooms attached to the main elementary schools. This brought about the charge of doubtful legality as the 1870 Act was supposed to cover only elementary education.

Around this time a young civil servant, Robert Morant, had begun to plan for the abolition of School Boards. In his campaign Morant had the approval of his boss Sir John Gorst, the Vice-President of the Committee of Council. Morant was working on changes to the English educational administration which he said was "muddled confusion without clear responsibilities, duties or powers."

Influenced by the 1895 Royal Commission on Secondary Education and studies of continental systems, Morant's report aided the Cockerton Judgement of 1899 which declared all School Boards illegal. This led to the reorganisation of the system under Robert Morant in a newly formed Board of Education.

During this period infectious diseases were common and in September 1899 Dr. Harwood, the County Medical Officer, called at Littleover School having heard reported cases of fever. So many children were absent due to the prevalance of what was then known as "Scarletina" (Scarlet Fever). It re-opened again on December 4th but with only 97 of the 157 pupils returning. At this time the Boer War had begun between the British and the republics of the Orange Free States and the Transvaal.

Early in the new century a recently appointed inspector, Mr. Fitzmaurice, made St. Peter's school his first visit in his district. He recommended better means of heating the west end of the large main room. The vicar called on March 1st bringing news of the Boer War with the "Relief of Ladysmith". On April 27th the children were allowed to go and witness a motor-car procession on Burton Road. This was the year that the Dunlop Rubber Company produced its first pneumatic motor tyre and the British Labour Party was founded by combining the Independent Labour Party, the Fabian Society and the Trade Unions.

On May 22nd 1900, the age limit for boys working in the coal mines was raised from twelve to thirteen. This was in keeping with Richard Morant's later policies on education when the higher grade schools were abolished and the leaving age became thirteen.

In September, children in Standard III were taken for a walk in nearby fields and were asked to note the trees, the crop of corn and the darting flight path of the swallows. The vicar called on September 27th to photograph the children for the first time.

In 1901 St. Peter's School received students from Derby Diocesan Training College for School Mistresses to witness the running of the school. These visits continued on a regular basis. Two unprecedented half day holidays were given to the children at the beginning of the year. On January 22nd at the age of 81, Queen Victoria died at Osborne House on the Isle of Wight. She was the longest serving and longest lived monarch in British history. The second half-day holiday was given on March 22nd to prepare the school for a tea and presentation to Corporal Morley who had returned from the Boer War in South Africa. Corporal Arthur Morley was a member of the Volunteers and had risked many dangers. He served with the 8th Company Derbyshire Imperial Yeomanry. Littleover celebrated his return in the schoolroom by holding an evening concert with Mr. Toft accompanying songs and a selection of music on the piano. Corporal Morley was presented with a large-framed, full-sized "platinotype" portrait of himself. The picture was taken by Mr. Winter, one of Derby's well known photographers.

Mr. Toft's last term as a Parish Councillor began in 1901, this time for a period of three years. As a Councillor he was elected to the committee which was looking into the provision of a juvenile recreation ground in the parish. The council only achieved this objective a number of years later.

The First Lord of the Treasury, Arthur James Balfour, was so impressed with Robert Morant's ideas on education that he asked him to prepare plans for the reform of secondary education. This led to a new Education Act in 1902 which replaced local school boards with a dual system of administration run by the new County Councils called LEAs (local education authorities). Balfour introduced the Bill into Parliament on March 24th 1902 and by the time it passed into law on December 18th he had become the Conservative Prime Minister.

The vicar of St. Peter's Church explained to the children that peace had been signed at Pretoria, South Africa in June 1902, bringing an end to the Boer

War. They cheered the announcement but this could have been for the granting of a forthcoming half-day holiday. A full weeks holiday was announced for
the coming Coronation later in the month but this had to be postponed for six
weeks owing to Edward VII needing an appendicitis operation.

At this period the Conservative Government was becoming unpopular,
not helped by Balfour's Education Act. The local education authorities were
given powers for both elementary and secondary education under the Bill.
The agreement between the state and the churches by which voluntary
schools would now be assisted out of local rates, brought about a passive
resistance movement led by the nonconformist churches. They objected to
contributing to the funding of Church of England Schools.

From the time Balfour began to explain the new Bill in March local reac-
tion was strongly divided and the *Derby Mercury* devoted columns of editori-
al comment about various meetings that were held in the area. The Bill was
eventually passed in December 1902.

The editor's comments in April of that year outlines the feelings of all
sides. The paper explained that "the man in the street" thought that there
was no injustice in the provision of forthcoming aid from the local rates for
voluntary schools (of which St. Peter's was one). The alternative being closure which would have placed a larger burden on the rates and added to the
running costs of all elementary education.

The Church of England diocese in Derby was partly under Southwell
Minster in Nottinghamshire. In 1902 the Bishop of Southwell stated that "in
a very short time the voluntary schools would be placed on the same level
as those which had unlimited control of the public money and the rates." His
forward thinking took the view that the unification of the system of education should be a national one.

By the time the Bill had become law the letters in the *Mercury* were more
positive. One example came from an unnamed school manager stating that
"every honest citizen should do his best to aid in, and make it work out its
object."

The year ended on a forceful note for older children with the news of
the development of genuine grammar schools to be created by the new local
Education Authorities under the 1902 Act. These would admit children from
elementary schools on scholarships won by a competitive examination at
eleven years.

Important maintenance was carried out in the school during the summer holidays of 1903 when a new chimney was built and the bell turret re-faced. The interior walls were coloured and the ceilings whitened, new cupboards provided and an "infants' gallery" was removed. The "Appointed Day" when the school came under the Educational Authority Act of 1902 was October 1st.

HMI reported that new desks were needed for the babies now the gallery had been removed. These duly arrived on March 21st. Benjamin Toft the head teacher was having days off through illness during the year and in January 1905 he was so ill that he was under daily medical care and had to be confined to his bedroom. His two daughters, Edith and Mary, took over the running of the school with the help of monitors. Mr. Toft returned for a short period after his illness in May. He was present when the school was photographed in groups on June 30th but on July 31st the children were informed of his coming retirement. The vicar expressed a few words about the master's connections with the school and hoped that Mr. Toft would spend many years of rest in his well earned retirement. The children were

The date this photograph was taken is not known, but a sophisticated guess would be when the school was photographed in groups in 1905 and the teacher may be Miss Mary Toft the Certificated Assistant teacher at that time.

given tea in the schoolroom, provided by the head, two days before his retirement on August 31st.

The new headmaster, Bryan Daykin, commenced his duties on September 1st and the vicar introduced him to the children before they were dismissed at 10.30a.m. He wasted no time in assessing the teaching standards of the school and on September 15th he wrote in the Log Book that the children in the upper classes were very backward in oral arithmetic, geography and history and the school had made little progress in the new syllabus of physical exercises. He drew up a new time table with which he wished to experiment before submitting it to HMI for approval. At the end of the month he stated that the staffing in the infants' room was below the requirements of the Code and needed strengthening. He also provided a number of books for the use of senior children during the silent reading lessons.

Mr. Benjamin Toft died at the age of 65 on October 25th, at his home, Scarsdale House, opposite the school. He had suffered for some time with "heart affection". Sadly, a presentation had been due to be made to him at a public meeting in a matter of days. The parish valued his thirty five years of service to the school beginning a few months before the 1870 Education Act passed into law. The children were asked to subscribe to a cross in memory of the late master.

In November two new blackboards were fixed to the wall in the upper room and a football club was formed for the boys and a field provided where they could play the game.

A new assistant teacher, Mr. Wilkinson, was appointed in early 1906 and from the outset Mr. Daykin kept a critical eye on his poor time-keeping. By March, Mr. Wilkinson was spoken to in respect of his lack of interest and neglect in his work. The new headmaster was certainly making an early impression on how he wanted the school to be run. The caretaker was the next to receive a reprimand for not dusting the desks properly and for not obtaining the coal stock to keep the school warm when asked.

A piece of land twenty feet by ten feet was obtained at the back of the school in April for about twenty-five boys to have courses in practical gardening. This was followed in May by the innovation of swimming lessons for a few of the older boys at 7.00 a.m. in Full Street Baths. Mr. Wilkinson accompanied them and the boys paid for their own entrance tickets.

Empire Day, May 24th, was becoming a day of celebration in the country since it began in 1902. The school had lessons on the British Empire and citizenship. Patriotic songs were sung until the school closed in the afternoon.

The first term of the school year ended on May 31st 1906 and the headmaster passed on the results of his own examination of the work during the period. In the infants' (teacher, Miss A. Toft) he thought progress had been made and the children were bright and happy. He noted that a screen would be useful to separate the babies' class. In Standard I and II there were forty seven children in the class. However he was critical of the work in a majority of subjects apart from Grammar, Needlework and History. The discipline was very weak and the children were frequently playing and fighting with the teacher in the classroom. He complained that the noise interfered with the work in the upper room. In Mr. Wilkinson's class (Standards III and IV) of forty eight children there was a lack of thoroughness, attention to detail and the children were backward in many subjects. Only in Standards V to VII, with fifty one children, progress had been made; the children taking an intelligent interest in their lessons. Ironically, the teacher in this case was the headmaster himself!

The school closed on June 28th 1906 owing to the visit of King Edward VII to Derby. His tour through the centre of town included the unveiling of a statue to his mother, Queen Victoria, at The Spot. The statue has since been moved to the Derbyshire Royal Infirmary. He then attended the Royal Agricultural Society of England Show on Osmaston Park, situated close to what is now Ascot Drive Industrial Estate. The 3,706 acre estate was purchased from the Wilmots by the Midland Railway Company and included the hall, lands and growing timber. This was not the first time the show had been held on this site, nor the last. Part of the estate was used by the railway company to build their Carriage and Wagon works; here they provided a private siding for the King only yards from the show site. It was held over four days and the total attendance was 119,143. The money taken at the gate amounted to £8,432. On Friday, June 29th, the school closed again in the afternoon when the children were taken to see the show.

Various events took place in July 1906. The headmaster gave a lesson to the older children on the evils of juvenile smoking. Around this time Nature was beginning to be studied in school with several kinds of newts being kept on the premises and local grasses and rocks collected and classified. On July

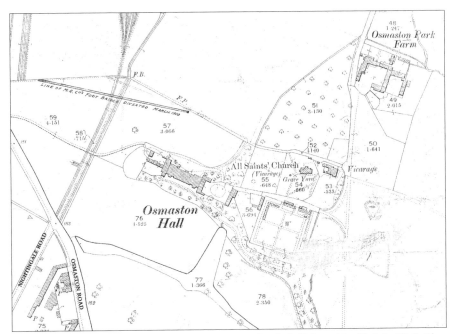

1900 Ordnance Survey Map showing part of the site where the Royal Agricultural Show was held.

7th thirty-nine children with teachers went by rail to Rowsley on a visit to Haddon Hall and Matlock. The parents paid the expenses and some of them accepted Mr Daykin's invitation to accompany the party. Each child took a note book and pencil, sketching and noting items of interest. A fresh water crab was found in the Wye and a petrifying well was also visited.

At the re-opening of the school on August 27th three new members of staff began; Mrs. Annie Daykin, the head's wife as assistant mistress and Daisy Broughton and Bertha Gilman, both aged sixteen, as pupil-teachers. The new Education Act (1902) was coming into force on September 14th with three children in Standard VII leaving to attend Secondary School.

Concerns were growing in the village about the increasing cases of diphtheria. Many children were suffering from sore throats or diarrhoea. A letter was sent to the Medical Officer drawing his attention to the existence of many reported cases.

On October 1st, Miss Katherine Jerrome, aged nineteen, commenced her duties as a supplementary teacher. She had been standing in for Mr.

Wilkinson for a few weeks owing to his illness but he terminated his employment on September 30th.

Mr. Daykin again examined the work of Standard I and II. Improvement had been made in writing, physical exercise and discipline, but other subjects were still weak. All in all he was fairly pleased with the progress under Miss Toft since his last report in June. He was now asking for a screen to divide the babies' class of thirty-six children from the older infants.

A window was found to be broken in the infants' room on 12th November and the desks disturbed. It was assumed that the damage was done by the Band of Hope children who used the schoolroom regularly and two evenings later many noisy boys were seen playing in the playground. Inside the school slates were removed from their usual storage place and a cupboard was disarranged.

At the beginning of 1907 the staff numbered seven, including two pupil-teachers. This went against Robert Morant's views that the pupil-teacher system should come to an end. However this aim could not yet be achieved as secondary schools were still in short supply. The first school to be "municipalised" by the Derby Borough was the Higher Grade Secondary School in Gerard Street, two years after the Education Act of 1902.

From August 1st 1905, pupil-teachers were only allowed to teach for half the school week and the other half was to be spent in recognised pupil-teacher centres. These regulations, according to Morant, would allow more time for general education during their apprenticeship. By 1906 a quarter of the school pupils who "qualified" to teach in secondary schools were ex-elementary school pupils whose fees were being paid by LEAs. However in 1906 the country was not prepared to accept secondary education for all children as a policy.

Arthur Johnson's father visited the school in February 1907 complaining that Miss Edith Toft had treated his son "unkindly". He was kept off school until April when his mother accompanied him stating that on a previous occasion the Stoppard boys had assaulted him on his way home. As two of the boys had left St. Peter's, and attended St. Chad's School, she now thought it safe to re-admit her son. Arthur Johnson was only seven years old when his father made the complaint. The Stoppards had returned to the village to live in Dark Street off Shepherd Street. There were four Stoppard boys at the school but they had moved from Firs Estate School in Percy Street, Derby. Three of them enrolled at Littleover in October 1905; Harold (11), Charles (9) and Jesse (7). The elder son, Alfred (12) joined his brothers in January 1906. By the end of that year Alfred and Harold had left to attend St. Chad's School in Derby. Their father, James Stoppard was a prominent member of the Derbyshire Agricultural Society. He died, aged fifty-two, on January 31st 1921.

On one of the vicar's regular visits he showed concern that the Education Authority had refused to pass a requisition for reading books. As a consequence the children in four classes had to share during reading lessons or read the same books as they had in the previous year. In addition he thought the so called historical and geographical reading books were more like text books.

Rewards for children were now becoming quite regular. Those who had not been absent for a year were presented with a deposit account with 5/- (25p) each in the Post Office Savings Bank, the Managers supplying the funds. Good attendance in any month resulted in a half-day holiday for the school and in June Mr. and Mrs. Innes, from the Old Hall, presented the school with a Union Jack which was hung in front of the class with the best attendance during that week.

At the end of the year an entertainment was given by the children with the proceeds going towards a Prize Scheme and the purchase of the much discussed screens between the classes.

In 1907 radical policies were provoking much discussion in Parliament. The Liberal Prime Minister, Sir Henry Campbell-Bannerman, opposed the Channel Tunnel Bill in March. The Bill was defeated because of the War Office objections and through lack of popular support. In June the Government announced plans to curb the House of Lords! In Africa there was a rebellion by the Zulu tribe against the British who were trying to impose a poll tax. This was also the year which would play a big part in Derby's development, with Rolls-Royce building a large industrial complex for the production of cars on Nightingale Road. A local company, Handysides, was chosen to build the factory laid out by Henry Royce. Derby was chosen for their expansion because of three factors; cheap land which was formerly a part of Osmaston Park, lower wage rates 33s (£1.65p) a week as against the higher rates at their previous site in Manchester and the number of foundries in the area which could supply components.

A crusade on behalf of childrens' health had been taking place in the 1890s, but it was not until 1906 that the Education (Provision of Meals) Act was put on the Statute Book. However this was without any statutory duty on the LEAs and school meals were never seriously implemented until 1941. A Government Bill which included medical inspection almost received a similar fate by a rejection of the House of Lords on the "grounds of economy and prudence." Luckily, a Private Members Bill by Labour MPs secured the Education (Miscellaneous Provisions) Act in 1907. Part of the Act relates to the medical inspection of children.

Under Section 13 of the Act it became the duty of all LEAs "to provide for medical inspection of children" for elementary education. At the local Education Committee meeting in January 1908 concerns were viewed regarding the costs, as about 32,000 inspections a year would be required in the County of Derby. The Board of Education had decided that not less than three inspections during the school life of every child would be necessary to secure the results desired. "If the work was done entirely by whole-time officers, it would appear that five such officers would be required and the cost (including travelling expenses but not including the cost of the school nurses) would probably be about £2,800 a year." The Committee agreed that whatever local arrangements were taken the work should be placed under the direction of a county medical officer and recommended that Dr. Barwise be appointed as medical officer to the Education Committee.

The school nurse visited St. Peter's Church School in January 1908 to examine the childrens' heads. This was to be conducted on a regular basis from now on.

Day trips were a feature in the school in 1908. Early in the year the headmaster, with two pupil-teachers, took thirty senior children to visit the Arts Exhibition at St. James Hall. This was followed in October by the School Managers paying for 127 children to be admitted to *The Palestine Exhibition* at Derby. The exhibition was held in the Drill Hall on October 17th, 23rd and 24th with many teachers acting as stewards. Tickets were sold in schools and more than 5,000 children attended.

An inspector's report stated that the cloakroom provision was unsatisfactory and on the girls' side there was no lavatory accommodation. The primitive closets for the girls and infants had to be emptied frequently. He

Littleover School photograph of 1908. A qualified guess would be that the Headmaster, Mr Daykin, is seated on the end of the third row on the left.

also thought a separate school entrance for the girls and infants would be a good idea.

Mr. Daykin's comments on two teachers during the year were again critical. He thought Miss Jerrome lacked class management and her punctuality needed to improve. He had spoken to her about being absent which left her class of babies at school with no teacher to look after them. He complained that Miss Edith Toft was a weak disciplinarian. The inspector's report of January 17th stated that the infants were under kindly influences but the children's interest in their work was not sustained and in consequence they showed signs of restlessness and mind wandering.

In February 1908 Mr. Daykin became the president of the Derby branch of the National Union of Teachers and in his initial address he referred to the aims and prospects of the teacher. He complained that after years of preparing for the position the average salary would be only £2 per week, while in other walks of life he might earn more. He knew of "excellent men and women between thirty and fifty years of age who were doing splendid work for salaries not exceeding £140 per annum for men and £100 for women." In the case of head teachers the posts were too scantily paid to attract large numbers of candidates. The head teacher in a rural school was even worse off, with a lower salary than his colleague in town. "He also had to manage with inferior staff and apparatus." Teachers had been lured into the profession in their younger days, he said, expecting much greater things later. They were now told that "it was not practical politics to pay a larger remuneration to the head teacher of a small school." The lack of due promotion for teachers after many years service, was in his opinion, the greatest hindrance to educational progress.

Another matter which concerned him was the state of school premises in some districts. Not only was more floor space required but also more playground was needed and more class rooms to replace the large room so often used for two or three classes. Attention should be given to cleaning, warming and ventilation in village schools. He ended his address with criticism about the lack of co-ordination between primary and secondary schools "and the many so-called secondary schools which take work less advanced than that taken in the higher standards of elementary schools."

Mr. Daykin had other skills. On Tuesday May 22nd the Littleover Singing Class gave their third annual concert in the schoolroom. Mr. Daykin was the conductor of the choir and he was congratulated on the success of the concert.

Report in Derby Mercury *February 7th 1908.*

Miss Toft, the infant teacher and her classroom, was still being referred to in HMI's Report in February 1909. "The room is an awkward one for teaching purposes and it is very difficult to give the youngest children a suitable school life. The Managers should consider the advisability of excluding children under five years of age. The registers at that time show that children of three-and-a-half years of age were admitted to the babies' class.

The inspector was scathing about the state of the school premises throughout his report. "Nothing has apparently been done to remedy the defects pointed out in the last report." He advised the Managers to consider means of relieving the congestion in the mixed school. "It is also very doubtful whether the infants' room is warmed sufficiently."

Two weeks later the Attendance Officer brought three temperature charts, one for each room. Mr. Widdows, the architect to the Education Authority also visited and inspected the school building on March 10th.

Cookery classes were organised for thirty-six girls on Wednesdays by a special teacher, Miss Nellie Symonds. They were held in the Institute, eighteen yards from the school, and lasted for two and a half hours. HMI of gardening was pleased with the progress the boys were making on their own plots in the school garden. "Some good habits are being cultivated as the boys are being trained to work outside the school with care and thoroughness."

Scholars were achieving County Minor Scholarships each year. Two, Florence Matthews and George Oliver, left the school for a free three year course at the Derby Municipal Secondary School in Gerard Street.

September 1909 brought more comments about Miss Toft's teaching. Mrs. Davies brought her daughter Dorothy to the headmaster showing marks on her upper arms and accused Edith Toft of causing these by pinching the child. Miss Toft denied it but other scholars were witnesses to the event.

The girls' and infants' cloakrooms were enlarged in September and a lavatory was added. The infants' room was also divided into two classrooms as the inspector had insisted. At a Manager's meeting soon after, it was decided not to admit any more children under four-and-a-half years of age owing to the over crowded state of the school. The problem was becoming serious as the number of children in the senior room was making work difficult and the air was becoming oppressive.

At the beginning of 1910 the school opened with 181 children present, twenty-four being promoted from the infants' class. With the infants' room now divided, and the youngest children being taught in a separate room, Miss Toft's teaching skills were able to blossom. The inspector noticed a marked improvement and said so in his January report. "The arrangement has greatly increased the facilities of the infants' accommodation for teaching purposes and it is now possible to secure more easily the attentive interest of the children."

This evidence points to a lack of decisive management, with insufficient attention paid to the inspector's previous reports. He was however pleased that the Managers had at last improved the accommodation with respect to the lighting, heating and ventilation of the infants' room, plus the provision of a new cloakroom for the girls and infants, with a lavatory provided. He was again recommending a separate entrance to the school for girls and infants as the only way at that time was through the boys' playground. The Managers proposed the idea to relieve the congestion in the mixed department of giving one of the infants' rooms to the older children. The inspector was firmly against this and told the school that more accommodation would have to be considered soon.

Attendance was down in February due to an epidemic of whooping cough, particularly in the infants and juniors. Ninety seven out of a total of 190 on the books were affected. Those suffering from infectious diseases did not improve in March, with cases of mumps being added to the figures. A letter from Dr. Barwise (Medical Officer for the County) arrived giving instructions to close the school until April 4th.

Four days after re-opening Mr. Daykin again saw it as his duty to speak to Miss Toft. This time he accused her of using the cane too frequently and frightening the children instead of teaching them. His term report in October was again critical of her and she expressed dissatisfaction with it. The head replied that the state of the infants class was not at all satisfactory as the teacher had not the necessary control for organised instruction and training.

The Derbyshire LEA received a letter from the Board of Education saying they noted with satisfaction that the Managers of St. Peter's Church School in Littleover were prepared, if necessary, to build an additional classroom. They had requested HMI to furnish them with a report on the accommodation during 1910.

The Managers later received notification from the Local Education Authority that the Board of Education had revised their assessment reducing the number of scholars from 218 to 140 older children and 39 infants. The Managers were told to exclude infants under five years of age and the headmaster should be held responsible for keeping down the average attendance within these limits. The Managers also asked Mr. Daykin to promote some of the infants to Standard I after the August vacation. This he duly did and

Littleover School photograph clearly showing the year – 1911. The teacher is not named but it could well be Miss Edith Toft the elder sister of Mary.

the average age of these children was six and a quarter but he felt that they needed another six months to be ready for Standard I work.

During September the school floor was treated with "Dustolio", a preparation which claimed to abate the dust nuisance.

Judging from the Inspector's final report of 1910 in December, no firm plans had yet been put into place for the enlargement of the building. He suggested that when eventually this took place the rooms now used by the infants could be more conveniently utilised by some of the older children. "The offices (lavatories) might well be converted to the water system whenever the other improvements to the premises are carried out."

The news headlines for 1910 were of the death of Edward VII on May 6th from pneumonia; Charles Royce, co-founder of Rolls Royce died in an air crash at Bournemouth on June 12th; Dr. Crippen was hanged at Pentonville prison after being found guilty of the murder of his wife Cora in January. This was one of the most famous murder hunts in our history, using technology in detective work for the first time; Dr. Crippen was arrested by the use of the wireless (radio) system.

The School Managers decided at last to take the necessary steps to extend the school premises at a meeting held on May 19th, 1911. The term examinations held during that month had shown that good progress had been made but the weakest subjects, arithmetic, writing and drawing were all in the infants and Standard I.

The school was closed for a week in June in celebration of the Coronation of George V. The local festivities included the presentation of mugs and medals to children under sixteen, village sports, a procession round the village with a band, free tea for children under fifteen and people over sixty. This was followed by a beacon fire.

Two new members of staff took up their duties in the summer. Ethel Daykin, the eldest daughter of the headmaster and Eva Margaret Phillips both were seventeen years of age and both began as student teachers.

It was decided to close the school for a week in August with the remaining summer holidays to be taken in September when the alterations to the school premises were to start.

The new building would take the place of the infants' classrooms and would provide forty-five additional places. This would create a central corridor, a new boys' cloakroom, boiler house and heating apparatus. The existing lavatories would be demolished and a new block built away from the

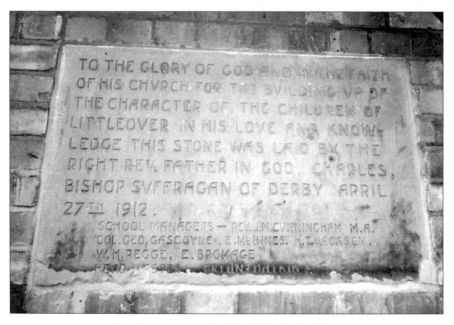

The plaque on the wall of the 1912 school building.

The eastern entrance for the girls and infants created in 1912.

The 1912 school extension at the rear of Church Street. The new toilet block was situated further into the playground.

school block, connected to the drains of the parish. This new toilet block would be between the extended playgrounds and the new classrooms. The latter are still in use but the lavatories have been demolished. A new entrance for girls and infants was to be made at the east end of the school; this too is still in use. All this work did not begin in September as planned but was put back to March 1912.

Mr. Hand, HMI, visited the school and inspected the premises proposed to be used temporarily during the school extensions. The building operations commenced on March 22nd with Standard I and II moving to the church room; Standard III into the Institute and the infants and upper schools into the main room.

Miss Edith Toft was again the centre of complaint during 1912. In the first week of May it was her designated turn to be at school by 8.45 a.m. to ring the school bell. She was late on three days. In June Mr. Evans complained that his daughter was afraid of coming to school because Miss Toft thumped her on the back so much while they had been in the church room. Mrs. Briggs complained in October about the mistress's treatment of her son Wilfred. Mr. Daykin spoke to Miss Toft about the matter. A month later the

Teacher	Status	Room	Accom.	At.	On Bks.	Average Age	
						Y.	M.
Bryan Daykin	C	A	59	vii	18	12	11
"				vi	19 } 55	12	1
"				v	18	11	3
M. Annie Toft	U	C	47	iv	29	10	3
"				iii	20 } 49	9	2
Annie Daykin	S	B	57	ii	22 } 41	8	2
Katharine Jerrome	S'	"		i	19	7	2
Edith M. Toft	C	D	60	Enf.	39	5	7
				223			

Extracts from the form sent to the Derbyshire Education Committee regarding the arrangement of classes.

vicar reported that he had received a complaint about Miss Toft punishing Nora Widdowson. Miss Toft stated that she did not remember punishing anyone. All these reports underline that parents were not always prepared to accept all kinds of corporal punishment.

Forty-six children, accompanied by four teachers, went on an interesting day trip on July 7th into Derbyshire. They took the train to Ambergate and walked about two miles to Crich Stand, the well known war memorial we would recognise today. (The tower with beacon light, 950 feet above sea level, was opened in 1923 as a First World War memorial to the Sherwood Foresters which is visible now for miles). From Crich they moved to the ruined fifteenth-century Wingfield Manor where Mary Queen of Scots was imprisoned in 1584. The master explained the uses of the various rooms to the children.

By September the new school rooms were being used and with the introduction of the hot water heating system it was possible to maintain a regular temperature. The County Architect, Mr. Widdows, visited the school on November 1st to inspect the new premises.

At the end of the month the school received notification from the Board of Education, signed by the Assistant Secretary stating that the intake of chil-

Supply Form 14.

Letters should be addressed—
" The Secretary,
Board of Education,
Whitehall,
London, S.W.,"
and should show the complete postal address and designation of the writer.

BOARD OF EDUCATION,

WHITEHALL, LONDON, S.W.

27th November 1912

Please write at the head of any reply—

1. Derbyshire
2. Littleover C. of E. School No.206

E.B. 24252/12

Rev. SIR,

I am directed to inform you that this School is now recognised by the Board of Education as providing accommodation for not more than the following numbers :—

Boys	
Girls	
Mixed	163
Infants	60
Total	223

I am,

Rev. SIR,

Your obedient Servant,

G. A. M. Moore

Assistant Secretary.

To Rev: J. M. Cunningham,
Littleover Vicarage,
Derby.

The document sent to the school informing them of the new intake figures.

The senior boys in 1913 in one of the new classrooms built in 1912. Mr Daykin, the headmaster is standing at the back. The old fashioned desks were replaced in 1915, but the cupboard on the left is one of a number that are still in use.

dren at Littleover Church of England School should be no more than 163 mixed and 60 infants.

The school continued to give half-day holidays to the children for good attendance but on November 14th a telegram was received from the LEA stating that the proposal to close the school on the following day was contrary to the regulations which stated that the holiday must be taken, if at all, within fourteen days of the last Friday of the month for which it was awarded.

Religious instruction was a very important part of church school life and the children were tested on their knowledge at regular intervals. The Assistant Diocesan Inspector, F. S. Boisseer was particularly pleased with the school in his December report of 1912. "The children answered readily, freely and showed an intelligent interest in their lessons."

The number of children on the books at the beginning of 1913 was 184 which was 37 less than the total allowed. The shortfall was mostly in the infants and Standard I and II. The staff numbered only five with the student teachers, Ethel Daykin and Eva Phillips, having left the school. The headmaster noted in June that the school was understaffed according to the code and two new members arrived at the beginning of the school term after the summer vacation; Elsie Parker, as a supply teacher, and Winifred Smith, as a student teacher. After Miss Parker terminated her engagement in November, Eva Isabel Bryan, aged twenty-four, began as assistant mistress. Her qualifying exam had been taken at Senior Cambridge Local in 1909 when she was nineteen.

During the summer vacation the lighting and ventilation of the main room were improved with the outside walls being plastered and repainting and decorating carried out on the interior. On September 17th the school was open for public inspection in the evening with the parents looking over the new buildings, decorations, and some of the childrens' work.

Many cases of scarlet fever were reported to Dr. Hogg, the medical officer on numerous occasions throughout the year. This led to low attendances, down to an average of 95.5 in June. A circular from Dr. Barwise arrived at the school in December stating that a School Clinic had been established at the new County Offices in St. Mary's Gate, Derby. This was received the week after Queen Mary had visited the Royal Infirmary in Derby.

A special meeting of the Derby Education Committee was called on December 22nd to discuss the report that nine assistant teachers from schools in the town centre had refused to take the children in their charge to see the Queen on her visit to the Royal Infirmary. The teachers stated "that they could not undertake to stand out of doors for an indefinite length of time." Teachers in the infants' department wrote asking to be relieved of the responsibility of taking children into the crowd. The Committee felt that the teachers were in "flagrant disobedience of instructions" and they could not in future expect to receive further promotion at the hands of the committee.

Troubles were gathering in the country throughout 1913. The Liberal Government under Asquith was trying to push through an Irish Home Rule Bill in Parliament. Lloyd George, another Liberal, had his house destroyed by a suffragette bomb and the leading proponent of women's rights, Emily Pankhurst, was arrested and charged in connection with the act. The House of Lords later rejected the Home Rule Bill and this was followed by Lloyd George saying the Lords should be abolished. On the positive side the first sickness, unemployment and maternity benefits were introduced and the first Chelsea Flower Show opened on May 20th.

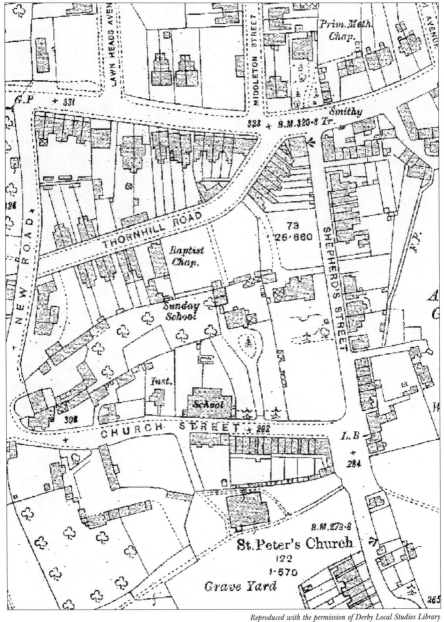

1914 Ordnance Survey Map which shows the school extensions of 1912. The toilet block is visible just above the main school building. The Headmaster's family home, Scarsdale House is situated immediately opposite the school. Sidney Road has now become Church Street. New Road on the left is now Old Hall Road.

The womens' campaign continued in earnest into 1914, but a build up of military arms in Western Europe was now the major concern for the world. Lloyd George called it "organised insanity".

HMI's reports were becoming more detailed and informative about how the school was or was not progressing. Mr. Hands, the inspector in January 1914, was satisfied with the way in which the instruction was conducted in the mixed school. "The conduct of the children and their cheerful and willing attitude towards the lessons are indication of the good influence that prevails in the school." He observed that the work on the whole rose above the average. "A good feature of the school is the comparatively large number of children who remain at school long enough to complete the work of all the standards and who thus came directly under the good influence and teaching of the headmaster."

Comment about the infants, unfortunately, was a different matter and is worth reporting in full. "The mistress (Miss Edith Toft) is kind and sympathetic in her management of the infants and shows much earnestness in her work but although she makes careful preparation of her lessons the children do not make the progress they ought to do and their attainments reach only a fair standard. Although they appear happy, yet they are not always profitably employed and their attention frequently wanders. Less formal methods and greater variety in teaching would tend to counteract their restlessness which so often exists." Suggestions towards this end were made at the visit and the headmaster was advised to give increased supervision and assistance in this division of the school. "The teacher in charge of the youngest class does not appear to understand infant methods and her teaching is unsuited to the children."

Miss Tofts became a certificated teacher in 1895, but many in charge of infants' classes were still untrained and known as "supplementaries" whose only qualification was to be British and vaccinated. Her year ended with criticism from the headmaster who reprimanded her several times for not looking after the younger children in the cold weather. He frequently found little ones standing in the playground and corridor with no hats or cloaks on them during the breaks.

Miss Jerrome the teacher of Standard I married in June and left the school at the end of July 1914. Horace Reginald Riley, aged twenty-three, was appointed as assistant master in August and should have started in the new term. However he went to serve in the Territorial Forces in the Great European War.

Britain declared war on Germany on August 4th after German troops invaded Belgium. Britain had signed a Treaty in 1839 guaranteeing Belgian neutrality and had warned Germany that it would honour the agreement after they declared war on Russia at the beginning of the month.

Two young ladies joined the staff as student teachers at the beginning of the new school year, Annie Daykin and Florence Matthews. Gladys Daykin began as a probationer for one month. Annie (18) and Gladys (16) were daughters of the headmaster and both had been pupils at the school. Florence Matthews had two sisters and a brother who were scholars at St. Peter's. The Matthews lived in Shepherd Street, very close to the school. Florence gained a scholarship to the Secondary School and then attended Parkfields Cedars when it opened in 1917 as the Derby Girls' Municipal Secondary School.

The Derbyshire LEA sent a letter to the school in July 1914 informing them that student teachers were required by the National Insurance Act of 1911, to pay their contributions. If they subsequently became certificated the contributions were taken into account in connection with the deferred annuity fund.

The health of the children was now taken very seriously. One girl's mother received several complaints by the school nurse about her child's "verminous head"; she was later removed to attend St. Joseph's School. The Medical Officer of Health notified the school of the growing number of cases of scarlet fever, whooping cough, chicken pox and measles.

Five children left the school to attend Derby Municipal Secondary School, on the advice of Mr. Daykin, the headmaster. Two others went to Hastings Street Higher Elementary School. This, according to the head led to only average attainments of the children in Class I, due to the removal of these bright scholars.

Many improvements had been added to the first Education Act in 1870 but what had not altered was the fact that it was still the working class families who were sending their children to elementary schools, the professional classes, apart from teachers, were still reluctant to include their children. Although the emphasis was still on the three Rs in 1914, the curriculum had expanded and talented children were now reaping the benefit. Individual reports on each child's progress were being sent to parents for the first time at St. Peter's School in 1914.

The oldest boy in the Matthews family, William Sheffield Matthews, obtained a scholarship from St. Peter's to the Secondary School. He went on to attend the Technical College and became a chemist for the Derby Gas Co, where he later gained a BSc in chemistry. He was in charge of coke ovens at Clay Cross until he became the Works Training Officer at Stanton Iron Works. William became a county magistrate and at one time was on twelve Education Committees. He served with the Navy in the First World War. The only record of the first year of the war in the school Log Book was the mention of the parents of a scholar offering a large number of cut roses. These the senior girls arranged to sell, with the funds going to the Red Cross Society. In November, with the war now three months old, four Belgian children were admitted to the school. Their families had fled from their country owing to invasion by the German army. The eldest was moved to a Derby secondary school in April 1915; the second left to attend a school for Belgians in Stroud and the other two from the same family moved to Islington in London on 7th April 1916.

Dreadful events were being reported on the war at the beginning of 1915. The first air-raids were inflicted on Britain when bombs were dropped on Kings Lynn and Great Yarmouth in East Anglia and there were many casualties. In the middle of February the United Kingdom recorded total deaths of a hundred thousand troops, by November they had risen to over five hundred thousand. One of the worst battles was in the spring offensive in Ypres, Belgium, when the Germans used chlorine gas for the first time. At that time the war was costing £2 million a day, rising to £3 million in the summer. In October a British nurse, Edith Cavell, from Norwich, was executed by a German firing squad for helping Allied prisoners to escape. There were lighter moments to report such as the preposterous sale of Stonehenge by auction. Mr. Chubb bought it for £6,600 as a present for his wife. Three years later, in 1913, he presented it to the nation.

Life continued as normal as possible in Littleover school with the proud announcement that twenty former scholars of the school were now attending secondary or higher schools.

Twenty-five new dual desks were provided to replace the old fashioned desks "which were unsuitable for children". A new partition was fixed in the main school room in July which made three classrooms instead of two.

A syllabus and plan of the school garden was sent to the Education Committee with the number of boys registered as fourteen. These boys became keenly interested in their gardens and often went to work in them during the evenings. The gardens were inspected in the summer to determine the prize winner in conjunction with the local Horticultural Society. The gardening year ended on October 31st. Swimming classes were arranged for both boys and girls in June. Twenty-seven senior boys left school at 3.00 p.m. on Mondays during the summer months. They received instruction in Full Street Baths until 4.00 p.m. or later. The girls, unfairly, had to attend after school, at 5.15 p.m. on Wednesdays.

Another daughter of the headmaster, Gladys Daykin, began as a student teacher at the start of the new school year after serving as a probationer. Her sister, Annie Daykin and Florence Matthews had completed their first year's training as student teachers at the end of July.

A "Red Cross Day" was held in the school in October when the older girls sold flags and the gardening boys gave peas and apples to be sold in aid of the Society. The children were addressed by the head who gave a talk on "Trafalgar" (October 21st 1805) and on the present day (October 21st 1915).

On January 31st 1916 German airships passed over the district and dropped bombs on Burton and Derby, damaging property at both places. Letters were appearing in the *Derby Mercury* after the Zeplin raid questioning why no steps had been taken by the Home Office to restrict lighting in towns and villages. Neither had any system been devised to give warnings such as a siren. A Frenchman, now living in the district suggested that several bugles could be blown, as they were in France. A Mickleover resident pointed out that the thirty lights on the platforms of the railway station were an obvious sign to the enemy. "The engines of the airships could be plainly heard, lights were shining out from some windows for many yards, in some cases the trouble not being taken to even draw the window blinds."

Horace Riley, the assistant master, who had not begun his term at St. Peter's in 1914 due to being called-up to join the army, returned briefly on February 14th and while on leave assisted in the teaching. This was the year when 420,000 British soldiers perished in the Battle of the Somme on the western front. This was a fruitless attempt to relieve the French as only ten miles were gained from the German army.

Mr. Riley returned to the school on a full-time basis on August 28th, having received his discharge from the army. He had to take time off later in the year to attend a medical examination at Normanton Barracks.

Students from the Diocesan Training College for school mistresses were still visiting the school as part of their studies. A party of thirteen senior scholars visited the College on May 13th to hear the students give a performance of *Richard III* by William Shakespeare. In the same month the headmaster was absent from school, being sworn in to become a Special Constable.

The gardening report by HMI on the operations taking place on the new plot of land was very positive. "Its site, adjoining the school premises is very convenient, but air and light are restricted on the eastern side by large fruit trees." However he was impressed with the enthusiasm of the boys who took pride in laying out the garden. "Their work does them much credit and the absence of weeds is a very commendable feature."

Educational opportunities were improving at this time with a remarkable increase in the number of children going to grammar school. There was full employment at a time of increased production for the war effort although the work was hard, wages were rising and women were working in the munitions factories which meant that working class families could now afford to let their children enter secondary education.

Widespread concern was growing for the children as unscrupulous employers were exploiting them in the drive to increase production. Herbert Lewis, MP, Parliamentary Secretary to the Board of Education was asked to be the chairman of a departmental committee set up to review the education given to young people after the war. In its Final Report, issued in April 1917, the Lewis Committee included an obligation on the LEA to provide continuation classes for young people between the age of fourteen and eighteen with the insistance that these youngsters attend such classes.

Regulations were issued in 1904 for the new secondary schools to provide a curriculum consisting of English, history and geography, an ancient or modern language, mathematics, science, physical exercise, drawing, singing and household studies. Unfortunately for the working class children in Littleover, fees were charged for tuition although twenty-five per cent of those who enrolled were supposed to be offered free places.

The historian, H. A. L. Fisher, was keen to catch the spending mood of the nation, as popular support was so high during this black time in the country's history. He introduced a further Education Bill into the House of Commons in 1917 which would abolish the dreadful "half-time" system which was still prevalent in the country, particularly in Lancashire and Yorkshire. Under this system children as young as thirteen spent half a day at school and then worked six hours in a mill or factory. His other aims were to introduce the compulsory part-time continuation schools for the fourteen to eighteen year olds and enlarge the powers of local authorities to promote all types of education from the nursery school upwards. All this was an effort to standardise practices throughout secondary schools. In addition the externally examined School Certificate was introduced.

Despite all this progress the majority of working-class children, excluded economically and socially from the private sector, still had only the LEA elementary school to rely on. The minimum leaving age still remained at twelve years.

According to the County Inspector of Derbyshire, Mr. Potts, St. Peter's Church School was rather privileged and did not seem to experience any deprivation. "The school is fortunate in having comparatively small classes each in a well appointed room", he wrote on March 14th 1917. "The children appear to come from good homes and have wider ideas and a more extensive vocabulary than is ordinarily found, circumstances which help the teaching of English and the development of general intelligence. In the geography lessons of Standard III it was noted that the majority of the children had visited the seaside – in itself a good beginning in the subject; the teacher builds upon the children's own experiences in an interesting and stimulating way." Later in the year eight children left to attend a Secondary or Higher Elementary School.

The next chapter deals mainly with the reforms in education which took place after the First World War and how Fisher's hard work in 1917 almost came to nothing due to vested interests a year later. Mr. Daykin had now been the headmaster of the school for twelve years, and his next fourteen were to be equally successful.

CHAPTER THREE

TEACHERS FACE CUTS IN SALARY
1918 - 1931

At the time of writing this book over eighty years have passed since the First World War came to an end but I can still remember the stories my grandparents told me about their experiences of this dreadful time when I was just a schoolboy, attending St. Peter's Church School. What I have discovered at this stage in my research enlightens me and enables me to take a more objective look at the school particularly of the teachers and headmaster who worked hard for the children of Littleover in difficult times and in the same classrooms that I, my sister and other contemporaries used some twenty years hence.

At the beginning of 1918 there was a heavy fall of snow in Littleover causing a very poor attendance at St. Peter's Church School. A quick thaw led to flooding at the bottom of Littleover Hollow and the children living beyond were directed across the fields on their way home.

Educational opportunities began to improve as increasing numbers of children obtained entry to a Grammar School. Although work was hard for men, wages were rising as there was full employment due to the war effort. Women were also working in the vital munitions factories which meant that working-class families could now afford to let their children enter secondary education.

At the end of January "The Tank Week" was held in Derby. Children from Standard III upwards were taken to a mass meeting of school children to view the tank and invest their War Savings. First called the "Land Ironclad" the tank was a new instrument of war. Invented in England and advocated by Winston Churchill, Minister of Munitions, it was first used in the First World War to great effect by the allies, which now included the United States. Over £900,000 was subscribed in Derby Borough during Tank Week.

Food rationing was brought into force in February 1918, beginning with meat. The school closed on the 19th in order to give instruction to the teachers about food distribution and to make out and deliver Rationing Cards. Pupils from the Secondary Schools and a number of clerks from the railway offices assisted in putting the meat scheme into operation. The Derby Food Control Committee faced many difficulties in distributing

THE NEW CITIZENSHIP.

Mr. Punch. "PASS, EDUCATION BILL; AND ALL WILL BE MUCH BETTER."

[By special arrangement with the Proprietors of *Punch*.]

The cartoon was reproduced in the Derbyshire Advertiser *on March 22nd 1918 by permission of the popular magazine at the time,* Punch. *Mr Punch, seen dressed as a commissioner at the Houses of Parliament, welcomes the Education Bill.*

rations week by week as the population was never fixed, soldiers came home from time to time on leave and restaurants had to be supplied. There was also a large new population of war workers in the area.

On March 7th and 8th the Committee concentrated on distributing Meat Rationing Cards. The scheme relied largely on the co-operation of retailers but the more affluent frequently ignored the system and ration coupons were rarely checked. George Spencer farmer and butcher in the Market Hall, Derby and Kirk Langley was prosecuted under the Maximum Meat Prices Order for charging three women prices that exceeded the scale of maximum prices. He was ordered to pay a fine of £12. At a Town Council meeting Mr. Smith asked for steps to be taken to charge the wages of the policemen engaged in regulating the queues to be met by the shopkeepers who were causing the queues.

Bryan Daykin, the headmaster at St. Peter's School, was on the Committee of the Littleover Food Production Association set up in 1917. At a meeting in February 1918 the chairman said the rumour that the Government intended to commandeer the whole or part of the produce of allotments was unfounded. Additional land had been acquired by the Association during the previous year.

At the Derbyshire Education Committee meeting on March 27th, 1918 a recommendation was made to economise on school supplies. Several members advocated a return to using slates to save on paper. Mr. Wright, representing the Derbyshire Teachers' Association, said that if the use of slates was again practiced he hoped the committee would stand by the teachers should a complaint be made by the inspectors, as they were against it. There is no record of St. Peter's taking up the offer!

Horace Riley, the young teacher who had returned after serving in the Army, was frequently taking time off due to sciatica, a painful back complaint. In April he terminated his employment with St. Peter's having been appointed as headmaster of Butterton School near Leek in Staffordshire.

Miss Edith Toft, aged forty-nine, retired from the school on June 25th having served as a teacher for thirty six years. There is no recognition of her long service in the Log Book, nor any mention of a presentation being made by the children. Miss Florence Elliott commenced as a certificated mistress on July 5th.

Earlier in the year Derby Town Council talked about providing facilities for physical exercise out of school hours. It was suggested that games could be provided in schools and playgrounds with the teachers being paid extra. The aim was to keep children out of temptation.

One of the members spoke of the forthcoming Education Bill and hoped that Derby would take advantage of the provisions in the bill to supply baths, gymnasia and play-time centres. Mr. Prince, another member of the Council, was appreciative of the Schools Athletic Association which was formed to promote football teams in various schools.

The 1918 Education Act became law in the summer when the President of the Board of Education, H. A. L. Fisher, brought in the minimum leaving age of fourteen and abolished exemptions of leaving at an earlier age for any employment, thus ending the "half-time" system. Fisher aimed to provide educational opportunity and facilities for all in the future with the most important part of the Act, the day continuation scheme. Tragically this section was in ruins after only a few months. Professor Dent mourns its failure in his book *Century of Growth in English Education* published in 1970, stating that "the collapse of the day continuation school clauses, remains a continuing discredit to our country."

Fisher, however, though was a realist and well before the Act came into being he said "no bill on education or on anything else can give a new Heaven and a new Earth" and although he was a true radical, the 1918 Act did little to provide better education for working-class children; their gain was to be taken in their own spare time away from factory toil. It was still a time when the working-class was expected to know its station in life.

The new scale of salaries for teachers was announced in June by the County Education Authority. It was decided, with the agreement of the Derbyshire Teachers' Association, to increase the salaries of headmasters from £135 per annum after five years service up to £350 for more than thirty years in the profession. Headmistresses advanced from £115 to £265 per annum. Certificated assistant teachers commenced with £100 for men and £90 for women with a maximum salary of £200 and £160 respectively for over twenty years service. Uncertificated assistants ranged from £70 for men and £65 for women and proceeded to £95 and £90 per annum. Supplementary women teachers received from £50 to £70 a year.

Teachers' pensions were also tackled by Fisher in his Superannuation Act in the autumn of 1918. A non-contributory pension scheme was to be extended to all teachers (except University Colleges). However, within a few years this was attacked by the Government.

At the October meeting of the Derbyshire Education Committee Mr. Wright (representing the Derbyshire Teachers Association on the committee) said that the teachers were very dissatisfied with the new pay scales because, they felt they were bearing a much heavier burden in connection with the war than the rest of the community. They observed that farmers and manufacturers, mine owners and traders were all in a more prosperous way. Mr. Wright noticed "that boys three months after leaving school were earning more than their former teachers." It was stated that the increase was something in the region of thirty per cent but Mr. Wright said in his case the addition to his income was only seventeen per cent. He quoted from statistics stating how badly the Derbyshire scale compared with other counties. Birmingham teachers were the highest paid in the country at that time. Headmasters with an average attendance of seven hundred were receiving £500 per annum and lower down the scale those with an an average attendance of one hundred received £360.

Head teachers found it difficult to improve their careers in Derbyshire. The pay scale could be better in Derby Borough but they were not able to apply for these vacancies as the Derby Education Committee had a policy that only qualified teachers in the Borough could apply. The only way heads could advance was by obtaining assistants' posts and re-applying for a headship later.

The chairman said the committee had consulted the teachers when the scales were prepared and the difference appeared small. Alderman Slater and Alderman White took the view "that the ratepayers had hardships to bear and the increase in rates would fall on many people who could ill afford it." Alderman Andrews thought that if Derbyshire paid less than other counties they could not expect to have the best teachers.

Several children were reported absent during the third week of July suffering from Influenza. This was the beginning of what became a very serious outbreak which spread throughout Europe. In October thirty-seven children were ill with the disease and the school was closed for a fortnight by order of the Medical Officer, opening again on November 11th.

There were still thirty-five children away from school on this very eventful day. At 11.30 a.m. news was received that Germany had been granted an armistice after signing what amounted to a surrender. Two hours later the children were granted a half day holiday to celebrate the end of the war. At 6.00 p.m. a bonfire was lit on the school playing field and an effigy of the Kaiser, the German leader, was burnt.

The school was closed again for five days due to Influenza and when it re-opened on 19th November the headmaster and his wife were absent, confined to bed with the illness. The newly-appointed teacher, Florence Elliott, took charge of the school bringing in Mrs. Heath (née Jerrome), now a supply teacher, to take Mrs. Daykin's class. Miss. Elliott became a victim of Influenza at the beginning of December when the number of children suffering had risen to sixty. Dr. Barwise was left with no option but to close the school again until after the Christmas holidays. The headmaster, Mrs. Daykin, Mary Toft, Miss Bryan took the opportunity to complete the school records and mark composition exercises. A number of exercise books were posted to Miss Elliott at her Clay Cross home to correct by the time the school re-opened on 6th January 1919.

Derbyshire Education Committee reported in December that half of the three hundred and eighty schools were closed due to influenza. At the same meeting it was announced a war bonus of 7s 6d (38p) per week for Masters and 5s (25p) for mistresses (not including student teachers, pupil-teachers and other young people in training). Mr. Wright, the teachers' representative, declared that teachers would not be satisfied with this concession but added, "half a loaf is better than no bread". The chairman replied that it would cost £10,300 up to the end of the financial year and would absorb the whole of the committee's estimated balance.

Influenza had spread throughout Europe in 1918, becoming known as "Spanish Flu". The reasoning behind this is thought to go back to the first known reports of such a disease in 1515. When figures were finally calculated, more people died of Spanish Flu than those killed during the First World War. Compared with other European countries, Britain escaped a great loss of life as against those killed in battle. The Admission Register at St. Peter's records no children dying of the disease.

In January 1919 the Derbyshire Teachers' Association made a vigorous protest about their salary scales and appealed to the Derbyshire Education Committee on behalf of teachers aged fifty five or more.

Illness was still affecting the school attendance into 1919, including teachers so the headmaster called on his son, Thomas Daykin to help out for a fortnight in March. Thomas began his school life at St. Peter's in 1906 at the age of four. He left in 1914 to attend secondary school and at the age of seventeen he is described in the Log Book as a Cadet.

At the Derby Certificated Teachers' Association meeting in April 1919, Miss Clamp gave her presidential address saying "that during this period of transition there was no problem so great for teachers as how best to equip the children for their parts in the battle of life." She went on "Central Schools were being established in Derby in large numbers but the association must watch jealously that their facilities were used to the best possible advantage."

A greater number of out-of-school visits were organised during 1919 beginning with Miss Bryan taking eighteen children from Class III to see the pictorial illustrations of *The Blue Bird*, a book they were reading at school. Ninety five children were escorted to a matinee performance of Lord Sanger's Circus who were performing at Derby during May. It was held in the Cattle Market (now a large road complex leading to a bridge over the river Derwent) for one day only. Children were admitted to the matinee for 4d (2p) plus entertainments tax. The annual visit into Derbyshire took place in June, this time a party of children went by train to Dovedale, accompanied by the headmaster, Mrs. Heath and Miss Bryan. A month later they visited Matlock where they examined old lead mines and two caves. Mrs. Daykin and Mrs. Heath also took thirty nine children from Standards I and II to observe the river and the bridge at Swarkestone.

The children were involved in the victory celebrations organised in the school and village. Two days after the peace treaty was signed on 30th June at Versailles the whole school assembled to sing patriotic songs. Carrying flags the children walked round Littleover in procession to the playing field where sports were held. On July 19th "National Peace Rejoicings" were celebrated with sports, a procession and tea, followed by a presentation of medals to all the children. Mr. Daykin was elected general secretary of the organising committee of Littleover's celebration and with the loan of a field by Mr. Clewes they were able to include al fresco refreshments and band concerts plus fireworks as attractions for the day. It was decided to arrange a dinner for the discharged men of the forces and a tea for the older people at a later date.

Phyllis May Hardy, aged five started school in Miss Mary Toft's class in 1919. Seventy six years later, in 1995, she wrote to the school describing some of her experiences. She explained that the school day began with all the school singing a hymn, the one she remembered well was *When Morning Gilds the Skies.* This was followed by prayers. The children then returned to their separate class rooms for a scripture lesson, occasionally drawing maps from the Bible which referred to the places they were studying. On a Saints Day the children were taken in line across to the Church for a small service given by the Vicar, Rev. C. R. Brown, and then taken back to their lessons.

Empire Day was celebrated with prizes being presented to those children who had received the highest marks on all subjects. One also was given to the boy or girl who had been the most courteous during the year.

Phyllis writes: "On that day Miss Jerrome, who lived at the top of Church Street, would ask us to take bunches of daisies which we gathered out of the fields. She would pack them and send them to children in London who were unable to go to the countryside and see them growing."

On Friday mornings the senior girls would walk to the Church Hall, then at the top of Shepherd Street, for a cookery class. They were joined by girls from Mickleover School, who had to walk a considerable distance as there was no transport. When the girls had sewing class the boys went into the gardens or to a woodwork class. "During the last two years we were taught how to use a hand sewing machine and make a garment of our own choice."

She remembers an old gun being on the playing field where the girls played netball or were taught country dancing. The annual "Garden Party" was held either on the Vicarage lawn in Normanton Lane, close to the playing field, or at the Coppice then owned by Mr. Russell. The Coppice was situated on the corner of Chain Lane and Burton Road. It later became a hotel, but more recently it has become a housing estate, after the hall was mysteriously destroyed by fire only weeks before building began. The girls, all dressed in white blouses, navy gym slips, black stockings and black plimsoles, gave a display of some of the dances they had learned. Phyllis looked forward to Christmas when the children gave a concert for parents and friends. "I am sure my mother got tired of listening to me rehearsing my lines and singing the tunes we had to practice at home before the big day." Other memories of her school life include a walking stick being used as a cane on anyone who mis-behaved; a blacksmith's in Littleover at that time (see map, page 56); and Strutt's the sweet shop at the bottom of Church Street.

In 1919 Fisher, the President of the Board of Education, established a Committee under Viscount Burnham, the purpose of which was to negotiate national salary scales for teachers in Elementary Schools. The teachers were represented by their associations and the employers by the LEAs. In October the teachers made it public knowledge that they were asking for their salaries to be doubled as they were still at pre-war levels.

A Departmental Committee had already agreed in 1917 that a recruitment campaign for trained teachers of good quality would be needed as only a proportion of those who had been on active service would return to schools. This was considered to be important as the school-leaving age had been raised and compulsory attendance at continuation schools would put new demands on teachers. The Burnham Committee recommended different salary scales for certificated, uncertificated teachers along with head teachers. These new scales were eventually agreed. Although not over generous they set the principle that they were negotiable between the employers and the employed.

The County Inspector, Albert Potts, wrote a good report for St. Peter's School in 1920; the older infants were making progress in the essentials and the classroom of Standard I and II had "a bracing atmosphere". The work was well maintained throughout the school and the only small criticism he made was on Standards III and IV. "Although the answers of the more intelligent children in the middle standards show conscientious teaching in history and geography the certificated assistant (Miss Bryan) is recommended to increase her requirements from the remainder; her stimulating methods in physical training might be adopted to work in the classroom." Physical education was being taken seriously in the school with teachers receiving the most up-to-date syllabus handbook on the subject. However a later HMI, Mr. Shawyer did point out the grouping of Standards III and IV for physical exercises was not suitable as "the children are not trained in accordance with their capacities." The syllabus had been modified from the 1909 edition which was based broadly on a Swedish system of education exercises and on the British Army and Navy.

The Derbyshire Education Authority were asking for information on organised games and the use of a field at the school. Form E193 was sent to

Exercises from the Board of Education physical training handbook for 1919.

the County Offices with the following information. Field, one and a quarter acres; two hundred and twenty yards from the school (at the bottom of Normanton Lane); rent £7.10s (£7.50p) and other expenses raised by subscriptions; numbers using it, boys seventy six, girls forty five. Largest number at a time forty seven (twenty nine boys, eighteen girls).

The headmaster complained to the Managers about the school premises which had been damaged during a concert held on January 22nd 1920. Two back rests to desks were broken; ink spilt on a window sill; a castor broken off the piano; the corridor not swept and the apparatus used at the event left in the classroom.

Derbyshire Education Authority outlined its plans to set up a Teachers Advisory Committee at a February meeting. The intention was to widen the discussion between different branches of education and to involve teaching interests in Elementary, Secondary and Evening Schools. Nine representatives would be involved in this new committee and Mr. Daykin attended the initial meeting when various aspects were discussed from the value of scholarships to the granting of medical certificates to pupils who were absent from school. One example of the abuse of the latter item was highlighted when a boy in Belper was found to be attending football matches, the cinema and selling articles in the streets.

The policy of building new schools was discussed when Alderman Waite thought that they could be delayed in order that new houses be erected. Mr. Daykin contended that as there was no shortage of labour the responsibility lay with the Government. There was a general consensus that false statements had been made on the subject of housing by both the Ministry of Health and by the Prime Minister, David Lloyd George.

Mr. Daykin also stated that it was "absolutely necessary that home slum schools in the county should be replaced by modern schools." The chairman, Alderman Johnson Pearson, said "he was sure the Sites and Buildings Sub-Committee would not go forward with any schemes until necessary housing had been built."

Two new schools were opened in Derby in 1920, the first, a Council School close to the Rolls Royce factory in Nightingale Road and the second, the High School for Girls in a building on land given by Mrs. Walter Evans in what is now known as Darley Park.

A very serious epidemic of measles broke out at St. Peter's at the beginning of the year; it seemed to abate in the infants room by March; but spread to Standards I and II. By May 31st one hundred and forty one children were present out of a total of one hundred and fifty.

At 11.45 a.m. on March 12th 1920 a man entered the school stating that he represented the Ministry of Health and had come to medically examine the children. As he presented no credentials the headmaster contacted the Medical Officer and arranged for the man to return at 1.30 p.m. He did not appear again. A week later George William Mellor, a clerk from Tamworth appeared at Derby Borough Police Court charged with obtaining food to the value of 25s (£1.25p) by false pretences. He had taken lodgings in the home of Mrs. Taylor in Avondale Road, Derby. She was told by Mellor that he was a doctor from Guy's Hospital in London who was visiting local schools with the purpose of examining the children. He said that he would be in the town for at least three months. He also told Mrs. Taylor that he had been to Mickleover, Littleover and Etwall schools and had had dinner with the headmaster on each occasion. Mellor showed her a list of children examined by him on documents that seemed to be official. Mrs. Taylor supplied her lodger with food to the value of 25s (£1.25p) but she became suspicious and contacted the police. Mellor was arrested at her home on 14th March by Detective Sergeant Smith. The detective said that when arrested, the prisoner said "I'm not a doctor, but I've made these people believe I am." He

The heading that appeared in the Derbyshire Advertiser *on 19th March 1920.*

pleaded guilty and said that if he was sent to prison with hard labour he would lose his out of work pay. The Chief Constable, Captain Haywood said that the prisoner had faced previous charges of false pretence from 1910 and had been in prison on and off since that time all over the country. Mellor said that he had obtained his medical knowledge while serving as a stretcher bearer in the R.A.M.C. during the war. He was committed to prison for three months with hard labour, the maximum punishment the Court could inflict. Today he would have faced a heavy term in prison for attempting to abuse children and probably spent the rest of his life on the sex offenders' register.

On December 31st 1920 Miss Florence Verena Elliott terminated her employment at the school. She was now twenty two years of age and had been appointed as a certificated teacher on July 5th 1918. It was not until July 11th 1921 that a certificated teacher, Miss Gladys Mabel Kidger, was appointed as her replacement. A number of temporary teachers were employed during the first few months of 1921 and a probationer, Miss Alice Maguire, arrived in April. The Superintendent of student teachers, Mr. Ward, visited the school in October and observed Miss Maguire give a lesson and discussed certain methods with her.

At a Derbyshire Education Committee meeting in March the shortage of teachers was discussed. The Finance and General Purposes Sub-Committee was asked to communicate with the Board of Education to find out more details as to why Elementary Schools in Derbyshire were facing a shortage.

Mr. Daykin attended the Committee for a second time and made the point that due to discussion taking place in the press regarding the under-staffing of teachers, some explanation should be given. He explained that at a recent meeting of his trades union he had never experienced such strong feelings in regard to schools, "particularly owing to scholars in the upper standards having to mark time because there were not enough teachers to instruct them." He went on to say that Derbyshire was producing the teach-ers but their immediate neighbour paid higher salaries thus the teachers were leaving the county. As questions were being raised in Parliament he wished to know if steps were being taken to relieve the situation.

The chairman thought that what was needed was a fixed standard of salaries all over the country. The Board of Education had requested that a sub-committee of the Derbyshire Education Committee should go down to London to interview them in respect of staffing Derbyshire schools.

The trips arranged for the children during the year were mostly out of school hours. The headmaster took the boys in the school football team to play teams in other schools around Derby.

Two visits were made to the cinema, fast becoming the largest place of entertainment in the town. The first in January 1921 was to view the *Prince of Wales tour of Panama, New Zealand and Australia* at the Empire. The film was shot by Captain Barker and was a pictorial record of a journey round the British Empire in HMS Renown. The *Sporting Life* thought "everybody should regard it as a duty to see it." The Empire Cinema situated in Becketwell Lane, Derby, was the second purpose built cinema in the town which first opened in 1910 as the Victoria Electric Theatre. Talking pictures had not arrived so the new owners in 1921 recruited a first class orchestra which consisted of twelve musicians to provide the background music. Three teachers accompanied senior scholars from 5.00 p.m. to 7.00 p.m. In the summer evening of July 6th about forty children went to see the film, *Christopher Columbus Discovers the New World* at the Alexandra Electric Theatre in Normanton Road. This cinema was later converted to the Trocadero Ballroom in 1953. The school was closed on June 29th to cele-brate another visit of King George V to the Royal Agricultural Show at Derby, two days later sixty scholars travelled by motor charabancs (coach-es) to Matlock, Haddon Hall and Bakewell church.

For the first time the Diocesan Inspector, Norman Louch suggested that hymn books be provided for children who could not bring their own. "It will then be possible for the children to sing new hymns after an introductory talk without needing to learn them all by heart."

During the last two years the country had fallen into a trade slump which led to hunger marches and strikes. Cuts in education expenditure occurred in January and August 1921 and the emergence of Labour as a third political party led to instability.

Teachers became very concerned in May 1922 when a Commons Select Committee met to discuss changes in teachers' superannuation. It concluded that the Government or Parliament had never implied a permanence that the provisions of the Act in 1918 should not be altered but that they should remain in place while the current salary scales were in force.

On October 13th the school was closed due to the General Election. The senior scholars were given special lessons on the methods of voting and the qualifications of voters. On the same day twenty-two older children were taken to an exhibition on life in Africa, China and India by Miss Toft.

Old scholars gathered at a social evening on December 15th, lasting from 7.30 p.m. until midnight. Five days later a social was organised for children from Standards III to VII and on the following afternoon about twenty-five parents attended a school concert. It was at Christmas 1922 that the BBC started to broadcast a daily news programme.

Two teachers terminated their employment at the school, Gladys Mabel Kidger (aged twenty two) in February 1923 followed by Eva Isabel Bryan who left in July owing to her marriage. She was thirty two years of age and had received her Board of Education recognition in 1910, commencing her period at the school in November 1913. The Vicar presented her with a beautiful English pewter rose bowl from the managers, teachers and pupils. Supply teachers were used as replacements until Doris Isabel Garratt (aged twenty four) who lived in Chaddesden, near Derby, arrived on 1st November as a certificated assistant. She was the first teacher to begin her career at St. Peter's with her salary of £192 5s 10d (£192.29p) reduced by five percent to £183 13s 7d (£183.68p).

An addition to the curriculum began in 1923 when Mr. Speakman, Organiser of Handwork Science Teaching arrived at St. Peter's accompanied by Mr. Hague from the County Surveyor's Department who went to recommend suitable cupboards for storing apparatus. The headmaster received the authority a week later to spend 9s 6d (48p) on "incidentals" for handicraft work.

The Conservative Party gained victory at the 1922 General Election with Andrew Bona Law becoming Prime Minister. He had to resign in May owing to ill health and handed over to Stanley Baldwin. His Government agreed to the recommendations of the Committee on National Expenditure, chaired by Eric Geddes in 1923 who suggested a five per cent deduction from teachers' salaries. The axing of eighteen million pounds from education expenditure also increased class sizes in some schools and cut state scholarships to universities. The Government had now come to realise that education acts were no longer regarded as sacrosanct and could be altered at will.

Handicraft became part of the curriculum in 1923.

Teachers of course regarded this action as a gross breach of faith.

Another General Election was held on December 6th only thirteen months after the Conservatives had gained a majority of seats. Stanley Baldwin was appealing to the country by prescribing protection as a remedy for economic ills. They were returned with a smaller majority, leaving the combined Labour and Liberal members outnumbering them. In January 1924 Baldwin was forced to resign and Ramsay MacDonald, as leader of the next biggest party formed the first Labour Government.

The teachers' concern for their future did not affect their dedication to the children's education at Littleover as they entered 1924. The Diocesan Inspector, Norman Louch, thought the same. "The tone of the school is very good and I am convinced that good work is being done." He recommended new publications by the National Society, *Scholars Self Teaching Guides, Lessons on the Life of Our Lord* and *The Way of Worship* which he thought would prove to be helpful and should be "worked through systematically".

Theatre and cinema visits were becoming a regular part of the school year, forty three children were taken to see *The Great White Silence* on the afternoon of July 18th. Shakespeare's *Midsummer Nights Dream* was performed on November 26th when sixteen senior pupils attended in the care of Mrs. Daykin.

The headmaster, Mr. Daykin, requested to the managers to purchase a gramophone for the school for the use in country dancing. He also asked that the educational year end in July instead of March so that it might coincide with the Secondary School year. Both requests were agreed by the managers but rejected by the LEA.

The new Labour Government did not last long and the school closed on October 29th 1924 for the third General Election in two years. This time Stanley Baldwin was returned to office with a huge majority; Labour retained one hundred and fifty seats but the Liberals were reduced to only forty.

A larger concern for school closure occurred with an outbreak of mumps in 1925 when only eighty five children were present out of a total one hundred and thirty five; eleven of these came from houses containing a patient suffering from the disease. Things worsened in February when the attendance was down to just under fifty two per cent. These figures were reported to the School Medical Officer but the school remained open. At the end of February fifty four children were absent suffering from mumps and eleven from influenza. Schools were sometimes closed unnecessarily because of infectious diseases but in most cases, provided the same staff was available, smaller classes became an advantage for those children who attended. In this outbreak the attendance numbers were disregarded under Rule 23 as a certificate had been obtained by the County Medical Officer. Hence the annual average attendance was not affected.

The school nurse excluded Cecil Lee, aged eight and a half years as he had Scabies, a contagious skin disease. His step sister Irene Ford aged eleven, was also absent from school eleven days later. A message was received from the parents explaining that both children would be going to Firs Estate School. A letter was sent by St. Peter's to the head teacher of both departments suggesting a medical examination before admission. The boy was admitted but the girl was sent to St. Chad's School, Derby. All the facts of the case were reported to the Director of Education.

A number of accidents were recorded in the Log Book during 1925;

This photo is thought by a former pupil to feature Miss Newman, a teacher, on the left. If this is so it must have been taken in 1925 as she left the school in that year having only been a student teacher at St Peter's for a few months. The pupils recognised are [1] Gordon Haywood who left the school in 1927 to attend Derby Municipal Secondary School; [2] Horace Peake left in 1932 aged fourteen; [3] John Woodhouse left, aged twelve to attend Bemrose Secondary School in 1932.

Edith Armishaw, an infant under five years of age, met with an accident in the playground on 14th April. A broken school desk fell on her toe and bruised it badly. The headmaster's wife, Mrs. Daykin, was knocked down in the street by a cyclist on September 24th and in the following month, on October 15th, ten years old Thomas Waite from the Coppice, Littleover, was hit by a car near Stenson Lane on his way to school after lunch. He was taken to the Derbyshire Royal Infirmary suffering from internal injuries.

At the Parish Council election there were fifteen candidates nominated for seven seats. Six of those who were standing were rejected and the successful candidates were elected by a show of hands. The Conservatives left the meeting without demanding a poll. One village elector asked if the Parish Council was to be run on political lines but the chairman replied that he would deprecate such a method; they were there to select the best people.

Mr. Clulow, an unsuccessful candidate, asked who then was responsible for a printed postcard which read "Littleover Conservative Association, Parish Council Elections, Monday, March 16th 1925, Littleover Schoolroom 8.00 pm. Your vote and interest is asked for on behalf of the following candidates." He too demanded to know if they were going to be run and ruled by a Conservative Parish Council but the answer again was no. This was the year Littleover Parish Council asked the local authority for street name plates to be placed in the village.

The headmaster made applications to the managers a day before their meeting on October 13th about the introduction of electric light and for the gullies of the school to be cleared after the playgrounds had been sprayed with gas tar in September. The dust that had been thrown over the tar was being carried into the school and washed down the drains. The managers agreed to obtain information about the cost of the installation of electric light from the County Architect and the chairman, the Rev. C. R. Brown, promised to enquire why Mr. Daykin wished to purchase the *Children's Encyclopedia.*

At the next managers' meeting in December it was agreed to install electricity as soon as possible. They were pleased that the headmaster had made some improvements with more books and better private study for elder children after comments made by the Inspector at his last visit. He had also commented that the middle classes attainments (Standards III and IV), often fell below the average of the school. "Their teacher is painstaking but diffident in manner, and her teaching lacks stimulus." Student teacher, Rhoda Newman left St. Peter's on July 31st, having gained a place at Peterborough College. She was replaced by Miss Joan Mary Parker who, Mr. Daykin thought, would prove to be a successful teacher at the end of the year.

The question of employing married teachers cropped up again at the Education Committee meeting in November 1925. The authorities, two years previously had stated that there was a glut of teacher recruits coming out of college who could not find situations but the policy was changed to employ married teachers when there was no alternative. Teachers' representative, Mr. Wright, from Melbourne, said there were columns of advertisements for rural teachers appearing in scholastic papers and he could not see why marriage should suppose to have much effect one way or another on the efficiency of a woman teacher any more than a male teacher.

A profound change happened to Education in England in 1926. The

President of the Board of Education in the brief Labour Government of 1924, Sir Charles Trevelyan, assembled a group of people under the chairmanship of Sir Henry Hadow to look at the whole range of Elementary Education. The impact of the Hadow Report, *The Education of the Adolescent* of 1916 recommended principle changes, the most far reaching of these was to abolish the word "Elementary" and substitute it with the terms "Primary" and "Secondary". The former was to include children aged five to eleven and the latter children aged eleven to fifteen who would receive a Secondary Education in a Secondary "Grammar" School or in some more specialised Technical School. An important clause in the report was the extension of the minimum leaving age to fifteen.

The report was published only a few months after Britain's one and only General Strike and two previous financial crises. A Conservative Government was now in office and although the Board of Education welcomed the report, the country's unstable economy led them to turn down the recommendation of a school leaving age of fifteen on the premise that three hundred and fifty thousand additional school places would be required and at least twelve thousand more teachers. They thought that there were more urgent needs such as improving Voluntary School buildings and reducing the number of over-large classes. The less costly reform that Hadow recommended was chosen with the division of the all-age Elementary School into two schools, primary and senior, making education a more continuous process. It is interesting to note that defence expenditure at this time was regularly twice that on education!

In June 1926 Mr. Daykin was absent from school on Parish business. He was at a meeting to discuss the proposal by Shardlow Rural District Council to build more houses in Littleover. A resolution was put to the Littleover Parish Council by the Vicar, the Rev. C R Brown and Bryan Daykin, the headmaster which stated "whilst recognising the need for houses [it] disapproves of the scheme for acquiring the Charity Field by compulsion as a building site [and] desires that the houses should be erected elsewhere and that the Charity Field should continue as an open place and playing field." Forty votes were recorded in favour and twenty seven against the resolution which was duly carried. A copy was forwarded to Shardlow Rural District Council stating that the scheme should not proceed which proved to be successful. A further parish meeting was called in July objecting to the proposed extensions of the Borough of Derby into a great part of the village. A letter was sent to Shardlow Rural District Council "to take such steps as they may deem necessary to prevent Littleover's inclusion in the Derby Greater Scheme. This again was successful and it was not until 1968 that Littleover became part of the Borough.

Electric lighting was installed in the school during 1926 at a cost of £47.10s.0d (£47.50p) with the manager's proportion being £38.14s.0d (£38.70p) the balance being defrayed by the LEA.

Letting out the school for different functions after school hours led to damage of equipment. On the morning of March 21st 1927, nuts and screws from desks were found on the floor in Standard I and II room and several seats and back rests of dual desks were loose. The school was hired for a concert on the 18th but the caretaker reported that the desks were damaged by boys in the Sunday School.

A note in the school Log Book on November 2nd informs us that the headmaster was absent in the afternoon attending a Masonic Service at the Hallowing of Derby Cathedral. Bryan Daykin had become a mason in 1920, joining the Hartington Lodge. A year following the Cathedral service he became the Worshipful Master of his Lodge.

The Freemasons of Derbyshire attended one of the eighteen services which took place from October 28th to November 5th at the newly created Cathedral. The masons provided the altar and reredos and the service set apart for them was on Wednesday November 2nd. The Provincial Grand Master, the Duke of Devonshire addressed the members before a parade of the forty three lodges from the Assembly Rooms to the Cathedral.

The managers were informed that Miss Toft was due for retirement after fifty years "good work at the school". The school was closed on the afternoon of December 9th to enable the teachers to attend a conference at the County Offices, St. Mary's Gate, Derby, to discuss the recently announced suggestions of the Board of Education.

The school was closed again on March 7th 1928 due to the premises being required as a Polling Station for the County Council Elections and on April 2nd for the Parish Council Election. Earlier in March Bryan Daykin was nominated as one of thirteen candidates for the parish election to serve for the next three years. At a show of hands he received the second highest vote. On being put to the meeting in April a poll was demanded from the

Form No 6.—Rule 33.]

DECLARATION OF RESULT OF POLL.

Election of Parish Councillors for the Parish of *LITTLEOVER*
[or for the —————— Ward of the Parish of ——
in the year 19 *28* .

I, the undersigned, being the Returning Officer [or Deputy Returning Officer
duly authorised in that behalf] at the Poll for the Election of Parish Councillors for
the said Parish [or Ward], held on the *Second* day of *April*
19 *28* do hereby give notice that the number of votes recorded for each candidate
at the Election is as follows:—

NAMES OF CANDIDATES.		Places of Abode.	Number of Votes recorded.
Surnames.	Other Names.		
Borrill	George Wright	Kingstonia, Lawn Head Av. Littleover	97
Bryan	Joseph	Normanton Lane, Littleover	220
Clulow	George James	Windyridge, "	238
Daykin	Bryan	Scarsdale House, "	314
Fletcher	Thomas William	Normanton Lane, "	71
Hayes	Walter Sydney	Thornhill Road, "	296
Milner	Richard	Normanton Lane "	67
Phipps	Arnold	Lawns Head Av, "	204
Rudgard	Harold	Hillcross Close, "	269
Salt	Harold William	Huffen Heath, "	187
Stokes	Richard Edward	Hill Cross Av, "	43
Swift	Tom	Bantry House, "	291
Watt	John Alexander	The Walnuts, "	401

And I do hereby declare that the said *Joseph Bryan, George James Clulow
Bryan Daykin, Walter Sydney Hayes, Harold Rudgard, Tom Swift
John Alexander Watt*

are duly elected Parish Councillors for the said Parish [or Ward].

Dated this *Second* day of *April* , 19 *28* .

Ernest W. Pedley

Returning Officer [or Deputy Returning Officer.]

N.B.—The Returning Officer [or Deputy Returning Officer] must forthwith cause a copy of this Declaration to be affixed on the front of the building in which the votes have been counted, and another copy to be sent, by post or otherwise, to the Clerk to the Parish Council, or, if there is no such Clerk, to the Chairman of the Parish Meeting. If the Declaration is made by a Deputy Returning Officer he must also forthwith send it to the Returning Officer.

Parish Councillors Election 6. Printed and Published by Shaw & Sons Ltd , Fetter Lane, London, E.C.4 L216 S2274 (w)

Reproduced by permission from the original document (D4530) in the Derbyshire Record Office.

floor. The conclusion was the same and Mr. Daykin took the chair at a meeting for the first time in July and became vice-chairman in the following year.

In May Miss Mary Toft requested that she be allowed to stay on at school until the end of July or longer if desired. The managers advised her to write and ask for her resignation to take effect on August 26th. Mr. Daykin pointed out to the managers that Miss Toft's pension on her retirement would amount to £75 per annum, which he thought was most unsatisfactory. He asked if a gift of a substantial amount could be made. The managers decided to organise an appeal to the parents and others to subscribe along with themselves.

Miss Garratt was also due to leave school at the end of the summer term due to her forthcoming marriage. After interviewing six candidates, Kathleen Mary Lockwood of Denby village was appointed as uncertificated teacher in the infants beginning on 27th August. Miss Edith Toft, Mary's sister applied for the position of uncertificated teacher but she was turned down as she was already certificated. A second appointment was made in August when Miss Frances Bertha Jackson was appointed as certificated teacher. Miss Lockwood was to stay at the school for just over a month as she obtained an appointment in her own village of Denby in October. Miss Mary Elizabeth Reeve, aged eighteen, joined the staff as assistant mistress on October 17th.

In the winter of 1928 Littleover Parish Council sanctioned the moving of the gas lamp from the school gate and it was decided to replace it with an electric light.

Joan Gillett (née Martin) started school in 1929 and wrote to the headmaster in 1995 when St. Peter's was celebrating its one hundred and fiftieth birthday. She was living in Bedfordshire and wrote about her memories which included her teacher, Miss Jackson, introducing the class to Enid Blyton and reading columns out of *Teacher's World*. Joan originally lived in Chain Lane and walked to school four times a day, sometimes playing with her spinning top along Burton Road. Joan remembers Mr. Strutt's shop near the church gate and opposite the White Swan. "It was a veritable Aladdin's Cave." She also recalls the headmaster and Mrs. Daykin living in Scarsdale House across the road from the school.

One event she remembered quite vividly was the children rushing out of their classrooms to see the R.101 airship going over the school. The *Derbyshire Advertiser* reported that this was the airship's second test flight, passing over Derby just before noon on the October 18th 1929. A few weeks later it took off at Cardington in Bedfordshire on its first flight to India and crashed at Beauvais in France with the loss of forty eight lives, including that of the Air Minister, Lord Thomson. This marked the end of British interest in airships.

The school managers agreed on a policy of improving the skills of teachers in 1929 by attempting to select certificated teachers when the next vacancy occurred. Two students from Derby Training College commenced a three week course in school practice in March and in May Miss Reeve was given permission to attend a series of lectures at the Training College; a supplementary teacher was employed during her absence.

The school was closed on May 30th as the rooms were required for a General Election. The Liberals helped Labour to gain a slight majority over the Conservatives. Ramsay MacDonald formed his second ministry.

Alterations and repairs took place during the year with two "Antifire Pistoles" (fire extinguishers) installed in the school even though the LEA refused to help with the cost as it was not their policy to install extinguishers in a single storey building. However it was a policy to replace all the worn boarded floors in the three classrooms adjacent to the street. Solid concrete with Granwood patent flooring fixed on top was completed in the school vacation. The floor was later treated with a special type of wax preparation with improved results. The managers enquired about the cost of the construction of a storage chamber underneath the school but as this amounted to a further cost of £100 this was put in abeyance. A new partition was allowed for in the school budget and this was fixed in position in October. Local Parish Councillor Colonel Rudgard paid two guineas for the old screen.

In September company shares fell sharply in America due to the Wall Street Crash. The London Stock Exchange felt the first shock waves in October and a general depression of trade began to take hold.

Local shop proprietor, Mr. Freestone, kindly presented an orange to every child before the school closed for the Christmas vacation.

At a special meeting of Littleover Parish Council in January 1930 the ratepayers were asked for their views regarding Derby Corporation seeking the powers to run trolley buses along Burton Road and Uttoxeter Road.

They wanted to create a monopoly eliminating any competition. A resolution against the proposal was carried by a majority of sixty five votes to four and a protest was sent to the relevant departments and to the neighbouring parish councils that were similarly affected. In the end the vote was merely putting off the inevitable as the tramcar fleet was coming to the end of its useful life. The electrified tramway route from Victoria Street to Burton Road ended at the 1930 Borough Boundary which was between Farley Road and Horwood Avenue. Only two years were to pass before the first trolley buses began to run up Nottingham Road in January 1932. They reached the terminus at Chain Lane, Littleover for the first time in August 1933.

There was a further discussion on the provision of fire appliances to be shared with Mickleover. The object was to acquire an engine and facilities for the joint use of both parishes and it was agreed to proceed with negotiations. A year later Mr. Daykin was among the councillors who met the town clerk of Burton-on-Trent eventually agreeing with Burton Fire Brigade to assist in case of fire. There was to be a retaining fee of £2 and reasonable costs in case of a call.

The recommendations in the Hadow Report conceived in 1926, continued to move on in 1930 with the new Labour Government attempting to raise the school leaving age to fifteen. This was again defeated on economic grounds.

The inspector reported that the headmaster at St. Peter's school was due to retire in 1931 He praised him for always being receptive to new ideas and "his quiet and persuasive manner has served him in good stead in dealing with the large numbers of children who have passed through his hands." The inspector, Mr. Young, suggested that a "newcomer" would care to alter some of the work by leading the children to a more sustained and ambitious effort. The two younger teachers, Miss Jackson and Miss Reeve were advised to cultivate a more forceful manner of addressing and handling the children. The infant teacher needed, he said, to "apply more extensively the individual methods of teaching now in common use." He added that both teachers were working conscientiously and gave the headmaster all the help they could.

In October the headmaster asked the managers if his wife could be placed on the Superannuation list. The Director of Education replied stating that the County Council had not included supplementary teachers in

Voluntary Schools in their scheme so no provision could be made for Mrs. Daykin.

Damage to the school was an annual problem for the managers, the local whist drives and dances causing the most trouble. Early in the year the promoters were asked to take care with the new partition but after the event nail holes were discovered in the beam supporting the screen. In November a leg of a large table was broken. A request had previously been made by the organisers to reduce the charges in letting the school. The vicar replied that as the chairs from the Church Hall had been loaned for whist drives at no cost, charges would only be reduced if the organisers paid for the hire of the chairs. Three panes of glass had also been broken during an incident not related to the whist drives and the matter was reported to the police.

Britain faced one of its most dramatic years in the twentieth century in 1931 when the American slump affected Europe bringing virtually a financial collapse. Although not directly connected with European or world events Littleover school faced a crisis in terms of its future.

The school opened in January with more pupils on the books than ever before. There were now fifty children in the infants room, despite five being promoted to Class III. One of the infant's teachers, Mary Reeve, left the school in April having accepted an appointment nearer her home. The school correspondent wrote to the Director of Education explaining that as there were now one hundred and seventy three children on the registers and a staff for only one hundred and thirty five, would it be possible to send another teacher as a matter of urgency. A fortnight later, not having received a reply, a further letter was sent to the Director asking for his personal attention to the matter, pointing out that there were several local ex-teachers in the area willing to join the school as a temporary measure. He replied immediately and suggested that as Mrs. Rawlins had acted in that capacity before, she should be asked to start her duties immediately.

Mrs. Bertha Hannah Turner, aged forty seven, was appointed as an uncertificated mistress in place of Miss Reeve on May 6th. A week later Mrs. Mabel Juliette Hudson was added to the staff as an uncertificated teacher. She had previously taught at Junior King's School in Canterbury, Kent and was now living in Burton Road, Derby. Student teacher, Robert Noble, was the final appointment of the year.

In the same month, Mr. Feek, Director of Education, wrote to the Board of Managers about a proposal to re-organise the school after the Christmas holiday, accommodating only infant and junior children up to the age of ten years and nine months. He also asked if the school preferred a headmaster or headmistress to replace Mr. Daykin. If the scheme went ahead it would mean a financial loss of forty five children over the age of ten years and nine months. The school was concerned that a decision was important, as the village was growing rapidly.

The policy of re-organisation led to an outcry in some village schools all over the country when they had their pupils transferred to other schools.

Mr. Feek attended the next managers' meeting and explained that there would be a difficulty in finding suitable accommodation for the senior children in Borough schools. After further discussions it was proposed that the school be retained in its present form and that a master be appointed.

The crisis in the country led to Ramsay MacDonald forming a Coalition or "National Government". The school was closed again for a General Election on 27th October the outcome being that the Labour Party returned only fifty two members against the four hundred and seven in the coalition which was led by MacDonald, thus making him virtually a Conservative Prime Minister, according to his opponents.

A committee set up by the Government in 1931 called for public spending cuts with education bearing the brunt. In answer to a letter from the Director of Education, the renumeration of all teaching staff at the school was reduced by ten per cent from October 1st 1931. Copies of a resolution were passed to each teacher. This was followed by a letter from Mr. Feeke stating that due to the need of national economy a reduction was required in the caretaker's salary. This affected Mrs. Lee by £1.6s.0d (£1.30p) per annum which she reluctantly agreed to.

At this depressing time Mr. and Mrs. Daykin's services at the school came to an end after being at the school for over twenty six years. They were presented with a pewter tea service by the teachers and children. The vacancy for headmaster was duly advertised and fifty one applications had been received. A short list was made for interview.

Bryan Daykin began his career as a student teacher at Riddings and later went to Saltby Training College. He became assistant master at Canal Street School, Derby and for six and a half years headmaster at Egginton. His wife, Annie Daykin (née Ludlow), a supplementary teacher began at the same time at Egginton but when Bryan became headmaster at St. Peter's Church School, Littleover, she moved first to Duffield and then to Smithy House. She joined her husband at Littleover a year later, specialising in teaching needlework. After retirement they continued to live in the village.

They both played an active part in the school and the village all their working lives. Bryan Daykin had volunteered to be a Special Constable during the First World War, acted for many years as a sidesman in St. Peter's Church and served on many committees, fund raising and helping to organise various events of celebration. Throughout his life he fought for the growth in children's education and was elected as one of the early presidents of the National Union of Teachers back in 1908. Although school life occupied a good deal of his time he was prepared to be nominated as a candidate for the Parish Council at the latter end of his career and served as a councillor for six years eventually standing down in 1934 when he was sixty seven years of age. In the previous eleven years he was instrumental in raising money for the Derbyshire Royal Infirmary and after joining the Freemasons he became a life subscriber member of the Boys School Charity. He died in 1947 aged eighty having experienced a second world war and coming through one of the worst winters in Britain, leaving one son and three daughters. His death occurred only a few months before St. Peter's School appointed its fourth headmaster since the school was founded in 1845.

CHAPTER FOUR

TALK OF SCHOOL EXPANSION

1831 - 1937

On January 4th 1932 the school opened at Littleover without a head-master. Mrs. Beatrice Williams, a certificated teacher, commenced as tem-porary headmistress and one of her early duties was to recommend a replacement for Mrs. Daykin, the wife of the former headmaster.

Robert Noble, a student teacher in the school was appointed as an uncertificated teacher to fill this vacancy. The Director of Education offered to help the Chairman of the Board of Directors, the Rev. Brown, to sift through the fifty-one applications for the posi-tion of headmaster. The managers welcomed the Director's involvement and asked him to join them at the interviews of six selected can-didates. On January 6th, after each applicant had been questioned, Mr. Chambers and Mr. Maxwell were recalled and it was resolved that twenty-six-year old Thomas Maxwell of Church Street, Pleasley, Mansfield be appointed. His duties to begin on March 1st 1932.

Mr. Maxwell was the headmaster when my sister Sheila and I began our school life at St. Peter's. Other familiar members of the teach-ing staff were appointed during the coming years.

Headmaster, Mr Thomas Maxwell

Following Mr. Maxwell's arrival his fresh ideas were soon in evidence. Within nine days he had organised a House System throughout the school and every child was presented with a house badge.

After the Easter break the Diocesan Inspector's fears of changes in staff were soon proved to be unfounded when he saw for himself the religious lessons being given in all classes. At the end of his visit he held a short con-ference with the staff to discuss a new syllabus which paid particular attention to the text and an explanation of the church catechism to justify it being a church school. "I note several things that showed that the headmaster is bent on cultivating an esprit de corps in the school and the scholars seemed already to be responding to them," wrote Mr. Pheasant, the Diocesan Visitor.

Various suggestions were made by the headmaster to the managers which included the installation of a wireless set (radio) in the school and the erection of a flagstaff. The committee agreed to the installation of a notice board and pin rails to display the children's work in some classrooms and for the school to hold an open day. The headmaster also desired a supply of Report Forms. His request was approved and the managers gave permission to order 2,000, matching the sample Mr. Maxwell had supplied.

The managers inspected the Granwood flooring which had been installed three years before in 1929. It had now lifted badly and a new floor had to be laid in August.

In Mr. Maxwell's report to the managers at the end of the year he asked for accommodation for woodwork classes and a toilet for the male members of the staff.

Throughout the world people were now experiencing one of the most disastrous and inglorious decades in history. The newly formed League of Nations protested about Japan invading Manchuria and there was a resurgence of German nationalism, culminating in the appointment of Adolph Hitler as Reich Chancellor in 1933. Unemployment in Britain had risen to 2.75 million leading to the Trade Unions organising the largest ever hunger march on London, protesting against the means-testing of unemployment benefits.

The serious depression in the country had halted the building of new schools. The second Hadow Report brought out in 1931 dealt with the education of juniors, albeit that it was entitled *The Primary School.* This concentrated on children between the ages of 7-8 and 11-12 advising teachers of the need of pre-adolescent children and suggesting what they should aim to do alongside them. One part of the committee's curriculum explained that it "is to be thought of in terms of activity and experience rather than of knowledge to be acquired and facts to be stored."

Mr. Maxwell seemed to be one of those teachers whose idea was to "read, mark, learn, and inwardly digest" as the Hadow Committee suggest-

"Jumping with a pole: The arms are used to increase the height and sustain the jump. A stout pole (e.g. scout pole or broom stick) should be used and care taken to prevent slipping". Taken from syllabus of Physical Training for Schools 1933.

ed. From the outset he sought changes, establishing a junior library for the school within a month of his appointment.

In March 1933 his previous request for accommodation for a woodwork class was turned down, the explanation being that provision for a district handicraft centre was being considered by the LEA to be based at Mickleover. On the other hand plans were being prepared and costs obtained for the additional toilet for the male staff.

The headmaster entered the school choir at the Derbyshire Musical Festival and they obtained third position and a second class certificate. The managers wanted to be placed on record their satisfaction at the success of the children at the Musical Festival. They also expressed pleasure in the arrangements made by the staff for the Open Day which had been well patronised by around one hundred and twenty parents and friends of the children who saw, as far as possible, the normal work of the school.

In 1933 a new syllabus of physical training was introduced by the Board of Education, claiming it was a notable advance upon its predecessor in 1919. The Board complained that physical education had not been uniform all over the country and in producing a new handbook it was hoped to offer expert guidance for the class teacher. Physical education was to include not only gymnastics, games, swimming and dancing but sports, free play, walking tours, school journeys, camps and all forms of exercise likely to create a love of open air and a healthy way of living. School swimming classes for boys commenced at St. Peter's on May 1st 1933 under the instruction of the headmaster, with girls on the following day supervised by an instructress. The new swimming baths at Queen Street, close to Derby Cathedral, was opened officially on July 30th 1932.

Staff changes included a certificated assistant, Ivan Ward of Tibshelf, Derbyshire who was selected from three candidates. Robert Noble left the school for Saltly College in September and was replaced by a student teacher, Mr. Castledine, for a six month period later increased for a further six months. His salary of £36 per annum indicates how the 10% reduction introduced in 1931 had taken effect when compared with Mr. Noble's first appointment.

In the last quarter of 1933 twenty six boys of over eleven years of age became the first pupils to join the woodwork class in Mickleover. The construction of the staff toilet was completed in November at a cost of £25. Further school accommodation was discussed at the Board of Managers Meeting in November. A suggestion was made that the Church Institute, next door, should be adapted for additional space as a temporary measure when the need arose. The Institute is best described as a tin hut on the western side of the main school buildings which was later turned into a library.

A small piece of pasture land called Constable field, fronting Constable Lane, off Manor Road, Littleover was proposed for sale in November 1933. It was agreed that if the field was sold the proceeds would go towards purchasing another recreation field. A committee, including Mr. Maxwell, was appointed by Littleover Parish Council to see if there were any better fields available. He was also appointed to an executive committee by the parish council who had the power to act at once to help the unemployed of Littleover.

The education authority was informed in March 1934 that the recognised accommodation at the school had been exceeded by ten per cent. HMIs Mr. Young and Mr. Blagden visited the school in the new year and spoke to Mr. Maxwell about a temporary building. This resulted in discovering what type of building the Education Authority would approve.

The County Education Committee informed St. Peter's that a new school for upper standards eleven to fourteen years of age was being considered between the Littleover and Mickleover area. The managers thought the opinion of the Diocesan Education Committee and the National Society should be sought. The Diocesan Authorities informed them that they could not make grants towards a school extension but a loan of £500 may be obtained free of interest. As the matter was becoming urgent a further meeting was arranged between the Director of Education and the architect.

Mr. W. G. Briggs, the newly appointed Director, attended a managers' meeting in April and was invited to send an estimated cost and information of the probable accommodation the school would require for the next seven years. Mr. Briggs said that no definite decision had been made with regard to establishing a senior school in the area. In the meantime he agreed that the Institute could be utilised for temporary accommodation.

In the summer of 1934 the Board of Managers agreed that expansion was inevitable and they proposed to send a letter to certain parishioners to try to raise the sum of £2,500 to £3,000 necessary for the proposed enlargement.

Mr. Maxwell took his public duties seriously and in July when he attended the Littleover Parish Council meeting he complained about the "misuse" of local playing fields. "Big boys interfered with the games of little ones," he said, "cycles and motor cycles were ridden on the ground, little children were bullied with pea shooters and prevented from using the swings. In fact the small children of Littleover preferred to play in the streets." Councillor Phipps said that the boys had been observed and the police had a list of names of the offenders.

St. Peter's School held its first annual sports day on the recreation ground, Normanton Lane in July 1934. In the *Derbyshire Advertiser* it was reported that competition produced some exciting moments. The four houses of the school, Grenville, Joan of Arc, Florence Nightingale and Captain Oates ended with Grenville winning by a large margin.

Work on the Institute was completed and opened on September 3rd with Standard I using the accommodation capable of holding forty pupils. It was soon evident that an additional stove would be required in the premises, the managers having to foot the bill for a smoke pipe.

A letter, dated September 24th 1934, was received from the Director of Education enquiring whether it was the intention of the managers to add to the permanent accommodation on the Church Street site. There was now a possibility that a senior school in the Littleover/Mickleover area was to be built as the Education Committee were in negotiation for a site for this purpose.

The Ecclesiastical Commission stated that land up to one acre could be given for the purpose of the school extension and they were willing to donate the ground which was already on the site. In view of this the Director was informed that the managers were taking steps towards permanent accommodation.

School life continued to run efficiently while all these negotiations were taking place. The choir was again successful at the Derby Musical Festival, gaining the Stanton Memorial Cup for two-part songs. A group of children was taken by the headmaster to a Schools' Concert organised by the Derby Education Committee on December 7th. This was to become a regular event. Music was a big part of Mr. Maxwell's life and away from school he was the conductor of the Littleover Male Voice Choir.

Staff changes were still being experienced in 1934 with many student teachers arriving to gain experience over short periods. Miss Madge Spencer from Ashbourne started as an uncertificated teacher in March and left in September to enter College in Leeds. Miss Freda Tunnicliffe of Woodville was appointed as a certificated mistress on October 16th. Some consolation for teachers was announced in the summer, their salaries would now be subject to a reduction of 5% instead of 10%.

School children were given a half pint of milk a day as part of a national policy to improve nutrition. Other government acts in 1934 were the introduction of driving tests and a speed limit of 30 mph was enforced in built-up areas owing to the large numbers of accidents. Steam trains however were aiming to beat all land speed records with the Flying Scotsman reaching 97 mph on November 9th.

The HMI report of January 1935 concentrated on the headmaster's achievements since his arrival nearly three years earlier. The inspector commented that Mr. Maxwell "has had to face the legacy of the old regime, a large increase in numbers and frequent changes in staff. He has therefore had to concentrate on organisation, on discipline and on working up a good standard in the fundamental subjects and he has had little opportunity for experiment or for developing the school in the way he is capable of doing."

Despite these difficulties, Mr. Young was pleased with most of the standards he had witnessed, apart from the teaching of geography, "which is dull and unimaginative and of no practical or educational value to the children in the top class."

He recognised that the headmaster had been working towards ideal standards in conduct and work. "It is now up to him to complete the preliminary work in the foundations by using his own particular gifts to stimulate the teachers and widen the interests of the children."

Mr. Maxwell was also having to give thought to school expansion and the movement of staff which was still taking place throughout 1935. He encountered other difficulties such as being in full charge of a class himself. This was hoped to be resolved by the managers making an application to the LEA for an additional certificated male teacher. Miss Lewis, an uncertificated teacher, joined the staff in January and, following the resignation of Ivan Ward in July, Hugh Whitaker was appointed as a certificated master from September 1st at a salary of £168 per year. Reginald Alfred Green, an uncertificated teacher, joined the school at a similar time at a salary of £106 7s 6d (£106.38p) per annum.

Problems were experienced in the temporary classroom; the Institute. In March the caretaker, Mr. Wootton, reported a smoke-laden atmosphere which was thought by the headmaster to be due to high winds and during the excessive heat in July he had to send the children home early with "the temperature being conducive to poor work and bad health."

In January 1935 a former pupil, Walter Bradley, of the Anchorage, Littleover was appointed Foundation Manager. He first attended the school in 1875 and said he had always been thankful for the religious instruction he had received.

The Board of Education asked when it might expect to receive definite proposals for additional accommodation. At a managers meeting in March the Vicar explained that an offer had been received from Mr. Thirlby for the use of The Towers, a large house on the western side of Blagreaves Lane, Littleover. The premises had been inspected by HMI, the Director and the Architect but the proposal did not meet with the approval of the authorities.

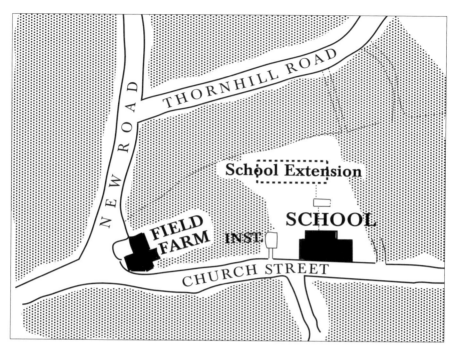

The managers were left with no alternative but to revert to the first site, a permanent building on Church Street.

In the meantime Mr. Bradley had been negotiating with Mrs. Rosa Lane for the purchase of the land adjoining the garden of the school. Mr. Bradley offered £50 but the lowest price she would consider was £100 and after further discussion it was proposed that the land be purchased by the managers.

Mrs. Lane and two of her two sons, Frederick and Albert, had continued the family tradition of working at Fields Farm since John William Lane began with seventy acres and the busy road outside their stackyard was a rutted path with two cottages outside their door. It was then in New Road, now called Old Hall Road. In 1936 there were only forty five acres and their cattle had to travel nearly two miles each day to reach the farm in the middle of the village in order to be milked.

All Rosa Lane's children attended St. Peter's School; Frederick John Lane was first registered in March 1911 along with his brother George Henry, before then they had been to the Board school in Normanton. Their brother Albert started in December 1906, a year before their sister, Doris May. When Frederick and Albert left school they both began working on the farm. George became an errand boy. Violet Ann the youngest daughter, started school in August 1916 at the age of four years and three months.

Doris May's daughter married Edward Ford and had two daughters, Gladys May and Doreen Joyce who were born at Field Farm but soon moved to Alvaston. Their two daughters, Gladys May and Doreen Joyce, began school in two different schools, Gladys at Wilmorton and Doreen at Brighton Road School. They returned to live at 1 Thornhill Road, Littleover and both girls began on April 4th 1934. Albert's son, John William Lane is a contemporary of mine and he started at St. Peter's on May 3rd 1943.

In June the managers sent letters throughout the parish asking for donations for "the erection of an additional separate block, comprising one large room for manual work and two classrooms, with the usual cloakroom, lavatory and heating facilities." The letter continued "failing this; our school will be classed as a junior school, and the elder scholars will have to go elsewhere."

Even with the generosity of Walter Bradley, who purchased the 900 square yards of land from Rosa Lane and her son Frederick John Lane, doubts were put in the minds of the managers after an interview with Mr. Briggs, the Director of Education. He said that although the LEA's intentions to purchase a site at Littleover had not altered, building proposals with the object of making provision for the future had not yet been put before the committee.

They were led to understand that if St. Peter's scheme was abandoned, permission would be withdrawn for the use of the Institute. However, if the school was enlarged the headmaster would be freed from teaching a class and the grade of the school would be lifted.

The Director was insistent with regard to the new school and stated that if it were necessary in the future to take away the senior scholars from St. Peter's the premises would be required for the juniors.

Members of the Littleover Parish Council thought the suggested enlargement of the Church School would prove inadequate in view of the rapidly growing population of the district.

At a special meeting in June 1935 Mr. Phipps thought the education rate was already too high and he did not think they could ask the ratepayers to foot the Church School bills. He also expressed the view that the attitude of the school managers was "dog-in-the-mangerish" and although they had their duty they must not be swayed by sentiment.

Mr. Hayes agreed and said that it was impossible for the church to maintain a senior school. Mr. Borrell declared that the church could not cater for a senior school as they had neither the staff nor the accommodation.

The Chairman, Dr. Watt, was a little more sympathetic although he was against a suggested scheme of sending senior scholars to Derby. The Parish Council had already recommended to the Education Authority to build a senior school and Dr. Watt informed the meeting that whatever was done with the Church School, the area would still require a senior school. There were sixty five senior children in Littleover and seventy five in Mickleover, besides those at Findern. Dr. Watt's opinion was that a senior school should be built and by the time it was complete they would be able to fill it. Mr. Baker thought the matter was resolving itself through the lack of support given to the vicar's recent appeal.

The Chairman reminded those in opposition, that if they expressed their views they would prevent the church from embarking upon an expensive and crippling scheme. "Yet men who gave their money for a cause like this were to be admired." A resolution was passed to recommend the erection of the senior school "with all dispatch", as an urgent need existed.

The Vicar and Chairman of the Board of Managers, the Rev. Cyril Rogers Brown MA, replied to all this criticism in the church parish magazine a fortnight later.

"It is important to understand that whilst the County Education Committee is recommending the County Council to purchase a site of fifteen acres down Pastures Hill, they have no plans at present for building upon it and they would only place a school there if and when it was required."

He explained that land was being sought within all areas near Derby with an eye to the future and the local senior school. This would eventually become necessary to serve the needs of Littleover and Mickleover but at this time the school at Mickleover was not full. However, he continued, the overcrowding at St. Peter's was a different matter which the managers appreciated would have to be dealt with.

Bertram Thorpe, the Board of Managers' treasurer and County Council representative was of the opinion that if they went ahead with the scheme they would retain the status of a senior school.

They decided to proceed with the collection of subscriptions and take steps to counteract the misunderstanding the press reports had created. An account was opened at the Westminster Bank under the title "Littleover Church School Enlargement Fund". In August the Vicar reported that £913 10s 0d (£913.50p) had been received for the Appeal Fund.

Some new admissions at the school in 1935 came from new building developments taking place in and around the village. In March the parish council held a meeting to discuss the village celebrations for the Silver Jubilee of George V. It was decided that entertainments would take the form of a tea or meal for children and Old Age Pensioners and some form of gift. A general committee, which included Mr. Maxwell, would be left to deal with the exact details. The school was closed on May 6th and 7th and a national holiday was granted to join in the celebrations.

The parish council followed the Jubilee success with a meeting about the acquisition of two fields at the sum of £1,350 for the purpose of laying out the necessary pavilion and other services for a further recreation ground in Littleover. They became the King George V Playing Fields off Briars Lane. There were already two recreation grounds serving the village; one to the east of Blagreaves Lane and the other just south of Brayfield Avenue.

Considering the building that would be taking place the Diocesan office pointed out that the school managers and trustees were liable for accidents to school children, staff, caretakers and outside persons through defects in the school premises and recommended that a comprehensive insurance scheme, offered by the Ecclesiastical Insurance Office be taken. The annual payment was 6s (30p) per school plus 1s (5p) per head for each teacher and caretaker. The managers were covered under a different premium through the Royal Exchange Company.

Final arrangements were made to appoint Messrs Currey and Widdows as architects who were asked for a draft plan of the enlargement which could be sent to the Director for comments and also to the Board of Education. It was resolved that the Vicar should look into the possibility of obtaining a loan free of interest from the Diocesan authorities and maybe a grant through the Bishop's Appeal Fund.

By December the plans prepared by Mr. Widdows were discussed and it was decided that the new premises should be built on the upper piece of land to the north. The estimated cost was £,3096 plus fees of $7^1/2$%. It was decided to omit the verandah and move back the boiler house; two rooms should be provided for the staff and the toilets were to be extended.

The school was open for a few days only in 1936 before the children were informed at assembly that King George V had died on January 20th. The school was closed eight days later on the occasion of the State funeral.

The headmaster asked permission to install a radiogram in the school out of the proceeds of the school concert performed before Christmas. Although the request was granted the chairman asked Mr. Maxwell not to make any future appeal for such purposes without the consent of the managers, particularly as the concert had raised sufficient money to defray the cost of the school party and they wanted to avoid too many calls upon the generosity of the parishioners.

The question of a senior school for Littleover was raised by Mr. Appleby at the parish council meeting in March 1936. The Chairman, Dr. Watt and the Rev. Brown, Chairman of the school managers explained what was already being done and that the parish council had put pressure on the County Council to provide a senior school. Dr. Watt joined the Board of Managers of the school in 1938.

A meeting with the Director of Education resulted in Mr. Briggs explaining that a grant could not be offered by the authority, as a government bill which would sanction such a move was only in its early stages. The more ambitious and revised new plan was considered but certain difficulties appeared in regard to the level of the land so the architect was invited to attend a few days later to discuss the matter. The plans which showed the new buildings joined on to the present school were discussed when the architect arrived. It was felt that the portion planned to be at right angles to Church Street (approximately in the position of the Institute) would be costly to erect owing to the marked rise in the ground from south to north. After viewing various alternatives it was decided that the architect should prepare a plan showing buildings roughly on the line of the northern boundary of the present playground.

After the revised plans had been sanctioned by the Board of Education the architect was instructed to send out tenders, to include the date of completion, to seven local building firms.

The number of children on the books was 290 making accommodation very difficult. The Vicar negotiated with the Baptist Chapel officials about the possibility of taking over their schoolroom. The headmaster was asked to use discretion with regard to the admission of pupils resident outside the parish.

The winning St Peter's junior team with the trophy from the Inter School Sports at Spondon.

Forty children attended the Inter School Sports Day at Spondon on June 12th. The junior team returned as winners of the trophy, the seniors being runners-up in their class. Junior girl champion was Margaret Hunt who went on to represent the school, along with seven others, at the Trent Valley Teams County Championships.

Additional temporary accommodation was still possible at the Baptist schoolroom. The use of the Grange which had remained unoccupied since Eastwoods, the foundry owners, left it was considered. The Methodist Chapel was suggested as a place for meetings which would relieve St. Peter's Church Hall for school purposes.

The sum of £70 was paid to Rosa Lane by the contractors for the right of way from New Road, allowing the transport of materials to the site. The contract insisted that all damage be made good along with the replacement of the dividing fence.

A temporary class of girls in the Church Hall was granted pending the completion of the school extension.

The building site activities produced accidents. In October a pupil

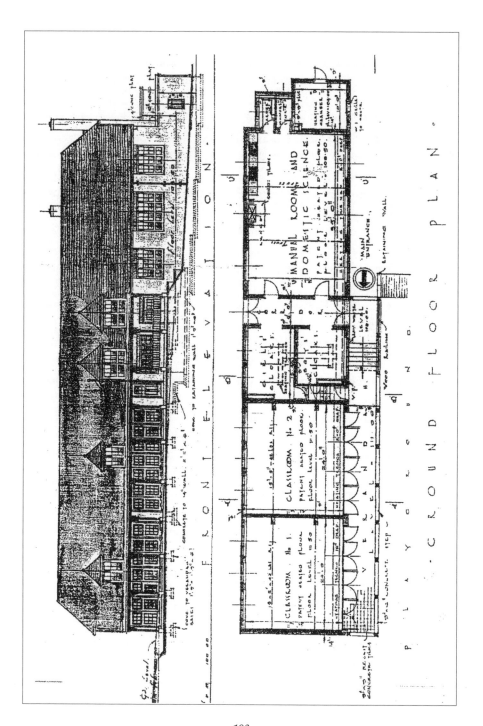

FRONT ELEVATION.

PLAY GROUND FLOOR PLAN.

CLASSROOM No 1.

CLASSROOM No 2.

MANUAL ROOM AND DOMESTIC SCIENCE.

MAIN ENTRANCE.

VERANDAH.

severely lacerated his knee by falling on the uneven surface of the new drain. More seriously a boy who had broken the rules stating that no child should enter the new building operations, broke his arm when playing on the scaffolding.

The Bishop of Derby had to decline the invitation to lay the foundation stone on October 3rd 1936 but Archdeacon Noakes promised to do so. A full day's celebrations were helped by the Mothers Union providing the necessary help with the catering.

This was another year of staff changes, although three appointments remained for a settled period; among them were Miss Madge Spencer who returned for a second period after her studies at Leeds College and Lizzie Grattidge as an uncertificated teacher.

An Education Act in 1936 raised the school leaving age to fifteen, to take effect from September 1st 1939. If the children had a job to go to they could still leave at fourteen. However all this was suspended owing to the outbreak of war.

The majority of the staff were unable to attend school at the start of the new year due to an outbreak of influenza, prevalent throughout the country.

St. Peter's received a new regulations booklet in April 1937 from the Derbyshire Education Committee. This cancelled all previous instructions going back to January 1925. One interesting rule which had been altered was the employment of married women teachers. The Committee had decided that no married woman should be appointed on the staff of a council school and managers of voluntary schools were asked to adopt a similar practice. A mistress who married had to resign unless the Committee's consent was given to the contrary. If for any reason a reduction in staff was necessary a married woman who was not mainly dependent on her earnings should generally be the first to receive notice.

Celebrations took place throughout the country to mark the Coronation of King George VI and the BBC marked the occasion by making this event their first outside broadcast. This followed the abdication of his brother Edward VIII who was now the Duke of Windsor and due to marry Wallis Simpson in June. The school was closed on May 11th and 12th.

The Education Committee would not consider the re-grading of the school until the new premises were occupied. There was a delay in completing the extension which was becoming a concern for the managers as

The foundation stone on the 1937 extension wall.

the dedication of the new building was due to take place on Saturday May 22nd.

The foundation manager, Walter Bradley, presented a piano to the new school as a gift and Mrs. Knee promised to provide a flagstaff. It was discovered however that she had been calling on parishioners inviting them to subscribe towards the cost which was contrary to what she had agreed with the Vicar.

The Provost of Derby officially opened the new extension and in part of of his address he said that "the religious education of the young was the corporate duty of every body of Christians. The history of education illustrated this to a remarkable degree."

He congratulated the population of Littleover on their good service to education. When the school had been built in 1845 the population was only 1,400 it had now risen to 6,000 and they had now "provided a building and equipment which met all the requirements of the Board of Education; £1,900 had been raised already and he appealed to all to use their best endeavours to maintain the church schools in efficiency for the days to come."

The Vicar, the Rev. Brown, replied that the school had been enlarged on other occasions and when they "again felt the pressure of the Act they had carried out the wishes of the Education Authority." It is now clear that the managers had suggested a bigger scheme for the school but the Board of Education stated that the one built in 1937 would meet their wishes. The school had received a loan from the Derbyshire Schools Association and one of £600 from the Diocesan Board of Finance.

Mr. Brown explained that the schools stood partly on a piece of the Vicar of Mickleover's glebe land and on a part given by Walter Bradley. The trust was held by the Rector of Radbourne and the Vicar of St. Michael's, Derby.

After the Provost had opened the door he was handed a silver key, as a memento. The new extension was used for the first time on May 24th.

Immediately after the opening and dedication of the new school the managers announced that due to the large expense recently incurred no further spending on additional accommodation would be undertaken. Moreover the managers decided that admission should be refused for any further children into the school in the lower standards. Older children would be admitted to classes where room could be found if they were resident in the parish.

The Education Committee agreed to place the school in Grade III from May 24th 1937 and this was followed by the announcement that the County Education Com-mittee proposed to erect a junior school in Littleover on ground adjacent to Blagreaves Lane. Mr. Briggs, the Director, attended a meeting of the school managers on July 13th 1937 and set out the ideas in detail. He explained that although the site had recently been enlarged there was still overcrowding and, as the population in the district was still likely to increase, land for the additional school was in the process of being purchased.

Until this new school was available the Committee proposed to open a temporary junior school and negotiated for the tenancy of an empty house called Blagreaves Oaks, which it was hoped would be ready for use after the 1937 Christmas holiday. The managers pointed out to the Director that the house called "The Towers" might be an alternative site and he promised to consider the suggestion. The Chairman agreed that the Institute would be made available as an additional classroom until the Christmas holidays.

The new extension at the top of the school.

Photograph of a junior class taken, it is believed, in the 1950s.

107

The meeting ended with an agreement that when the temporary school opened, children of junior age living in an agreed boundary attended there instead of St. Peter's.

In December fifty seven children were transferred to the Towers, which now acted as a temporary school, while the new junior council school at Carlisle Avenue was under construction.

The year ended with the old school bell being hung on the verandah of the new extension as a means of indicating changes of lessons. It had originally been in a state of disuse on the roof of the old block.

Only twenty years after the First World War, talk throughout Europe was about the re-arming of Germany under the Facist leader, Adolph Hitler. In 1938 large sums of money were now being spent on defence in Britain; £11 million on new RAF airfields; the Government signed a contract to buy 400 planes from the USA; 1,000 Spitfire fighters were ordered; the British Navy was mobilised; a national register for voluntary war service was opened and the Government allocated £200,000 to the building of air raid shelters. Two years earlier Britain had also been producing gas masks.

CHAPTER FIVE

WARTIME: THE CHALLENGE

1938 - 1945

I was born at the end of 1938 and became a pupil at St. Peter's in March 1944 but it was not until much later in life that I was to learn how far-seeing educationalists had been pressing for many years to achieve a more round-ed system of education than had previously existed. It has also become evi-dent that the slow evolution was not always attributable to the teachers but more often to the system in which they had to work.

Successive governments were, and to some extend still are, reluctant to fund all the recommendations of the committees they had set up; the notable exception in this field was the landmark Hadow Report produced by the Board of Education's Consultative Committee. *The Education of the Adolescent,* published in 1926 made far reaching suggestions for change in the elemen-tary school system.

The staff photographed outside the new extension in 1939. The back row left to right: Mr Banks, Mr Grist, Mr Whitaker. Front row: The first two ladies are thought to be Miss Grattidge and Miss Lenton. Mr Maxwell, Miss Jackson and Mrs Turner.

There are those of course who would argue that the under resourcing in education was because of the wider concerns of government; namely the depression of trade and the gnawing possibility of another war.

As far back as 1934 the National Association of Head Teachers held their conference in Buxton and one of the resolutions submitted was the raising of the school leaving age to 16. The speakers insisted that this would solve the problem of juvenile unemployment and reduce the figures in juvenile crime.

Mr. Biggs from London said that mass production was forcing the working classes more and more into a position of machine minders. "It cannot be too strongly insisted upon that education is the only antidote to the machine age. No thinking person can view with equanimity the inevitable results of a system where most of the people are engaged in occupations which ask little or nothing from the mind, and then spend their increasing leisure in equally brainless pursuits."

In June 1935 Mrs. Parker, a member of the NUT executive addressed a meeting of the Derbyshire Association of Teachers at Matlock and said "that the present system of giving scholarships and calling boys and girls to the front because they had done something better than their fellows was likely to be regarded as wrong in the future." She believed that "the great need was to make the child enjoy doing something useful in co-operation with its classmates." She went on to say that "generally speaking, the present system was calculated to turn out many snobs, whilst the real purpose of education was to fit the child for later life."

Derbyshire Education Committee was becoming more progressive and they passed a resolution to speed up the re-organisation of all senior schools with a view to raising the school leaving age to fifteen as soon as possible.

At the same meeting Mr. Hancock pointed out that only 16% of the schools had been re-organised. He said: "With the school leaving age at fourteen, children only had $2^{1}/_{2}$ years in the senior schools and therefore unless the age was raised it was doubtful if it was worth the cost of re-organisation."

The extension to St Peter's school premises in May 1937 and the subsequent improvements, were reflected in the HMI report of February 1938, even though attainments had been adversely affected by overcrowding and certain classes using temporary accommodation. The inspector referred to

Derby, Derbyshire and North Staffordshire Musical Festival

(COMPETITIVE)

First Class

This is to Certify that *Littleover C of England School*

gained *176* marks out of a possible *200*

in Class 10% *School Choirs (open).*

Thom Armstrong,
Adjudicator

W White

Marjorie J. a. Kidman.
Hon. Secretary.

Date *3rd March 1939*

---

the pressing need for attention to fundamentals at the Junior stage, although these were well achieved in Class 6. "The headmaster is fully alive to the situation and accepts it with the reverse of complacency."

Even though the prospect of war was looming, 1939 began as normal as possible; the school choir attended the Derby, Derbyshire and North Staffordshire Musical Festival once again. They successfully won the Brigg Trophy for mixed choirs. A hundred and one children, accompanied by the staff journeyed to Liverpool with other children from Derby schools. They made the journey by train and from the station travelled in sixty large buses visiting the Cathedral, Docks and the Port Sunlight soap factory. After tea they spent just over an hour at the seaside at New Brighton.

Confidence was still high in Littleover when consent was given in March for the Parish Council to raise a loan of £7,400 for the acquisition of The Grange on Burton Road. The plan was to build a Village Hall and turn the former stable block into a youth centre. The total cost of the scheme was estimated to be £14,150, £6,750 of which would consist of a grant from the National Fitness Council.

In April 1939 the school was informed of plans to use the lower block for ARP needs (Air Raid Precautions) but they hoped this would be deferred until the decision had been made to turn the Grange into a Community Centre. In the meantime the Parish Council was becoming concerned about undelivered gas masks, so pressure was put on the authorities to deliver them as soon as possible.

Under the Defence of the Realm Act the school was requisitioned for use as a First Aid Post on 1st September. Two days later war was declared between Britain and Germany, marking the beginning of the second world conflict in less than thirty years. On 13th September the school was closed until further notice although provision was made for groups of no more than twelve children to receive guidance and help in home studies from their teachers.

On 9th October instructions were received to re-open the school. The admissions had risen to three hundred and seventeen. This was chiefly due to a number of children, who previously attended Borough of Derby schools, demanding entrance to St. Peter's, now their schools had been closed.

In November Sir Roger Curtis, HMI, visited the school to discuss the accommodation, size of classes and the problem of more children awaiting admission; seventeen from the Borough and thirteen from the usual catchment area. The problem was not solved when the year ended.

The Diocesan Training College for Women Teachers was an important arm in education, housing as many as 150 students at a time, in the extensive College building or adjoining Lodges. Since the turn of the century students had been attending St. Peter's as part of their training, staying for short periods to experience teaching practices.

Interesting first-hand knowledge comes from Alwyn Johnson, a two-year student from September 1940. Born in Duffield in 1921 she first attended St. Ronan's School before the family moved to Northampton in 1931 where she completed her education. On her Father's advice she obtained a place at the Derby Training College, then rated as the second choice behind Avery Hill.

When she arrived most of the College accommodation had been requisitioned by the ATS and temporary quarters were found at Elvaston Hall,

Alwyn Johnson's Collection

Above, the baby room in the Practising School. Below, The gymnasium in the Training College. The school has now been demolished with only the old road entrance visible in Uttoxeter Road. The gymnasium is now derelict.

Alwyn Johnson's Collection

just off the A6, some three miles from Derby. This was originally the home of the Harrington family but they had moved to their other estate in Ireland.

Derby College was next door to the Practising School and in order to maintain the pattern of time-tabling, teaching and working with the children, the students were taken into Derby on one day each week to the Practising School. They had to take sandwiches, made the night before by the students on a rota.

The school was small having about 250 pupils in the Junior/Senior area. The infants were downstairs and the older pupils were upstairs. Children came from the immediate area, mostly walking to school. There were a few from Mickleover who came by bus.

Students spent a lot of time observing children and their behaviour and Alwyn's Education Tutor, Miss J. R. Thompson was a great believer that observations taught the teacher a lot about pupils, their behaviour patterns, background and psychology generally.

In the last six months of her course Alwyn had three full weeks teaching in Allenton School for girls. After being inspected on this as an examination, written papers followed before the final report and a mark was given as to whether they had passed or not and could apply for a job. If the student failed the teaching they failed the course.

Teachers were needed in both Derby Borough and County. All applicants were interviewed by the full education committee (approximately thirty) in the Education Office in Becket Street. Having passed the examination Alwyn was recommended for a post at the Practising School and after a second interview by the Board of Managers she successfully started work in August 1942 and was there for seven years.

In about 1942-43 school dinners were introduced at the Practising School and others. They were produced at Kingsway Hospital kitchens and were delivered in containers and placed on hot plates and into ovens specially fitted in the Hall. The Local Authority expected staff would oversee these but the NUT nationwide refused. Alwyn belonged to the NUWT who were working for equal pay for equal work. They did not refuse dinner duties, so being the only NUWT member she found herself on dinner duty for six months with two hundred children at a time. One pupil served the others at her table. This went on until the NUT had some time later reached an agreement.

From early in the war school milk had been issued in one third of a pint bottles for children to drink during their break in the morning. Milk was delivered each morning and issued to the children. This had to be done during the holidays as well, so on a rota basis members of staff went into school each day to issue milk. A school medical officer pointed out in 1943 that some parents who could afford the milk were not prepared to pay for it, although medically speaking their child would benefit from it.

Being a church school an examination took place on Shrove Tuesday when a parish priest was chosen to visit the school. As at St. Peter's each class was asked questions based on their curriculum. This was to keep within the law for the amount of time spent on Scripture.

Two male teachers left St. Peter's School in early 1940 to join HM Armed Forces and four air raid shelters were erected, one in the girls' playground and three on the playing fields in Normanton Road. The school was able to arrange "full dress" rehearsals in the shelters before the first bombing took place in Derby on 25th June. After the experience of the bombing raid, instructions were sent to the school to make shelters available to the public between the hours of 7.00 pm to 7.00 am.

Difficulties were still being experienced with the accommodation at the school, and no new entrants were allowed after the Easter holidays. There were still crowded conditions in the lower and infant classes but to help alleviate the situation application was made for Mrs. Williams and Mrs. Singleton, two part-time teachers, to be retained in a permanent capacity for the duration of the war.

The summer vacation was shortened to a period of two weeks by order of the Director of Education. When it re-opened the number of classes increased from eight to nine, a top class of twenty-five being taken for a period by the headmaster in the staff room. Certificated mistress, Winifred Mary Jagg from Scropton, arrived and this enabled Mr. Maxwell to return to his normal duties. He gave a series of lectures and demonstrations on *First Aid Instruction for the Ordinary Civilian* which had been suggested by the Education Committee.

The school "took cover" on the approach of enemy aircraft on 21st October. Guns were heard and splinters fell into the playground. The children were marched to the shelters on the following day for an hour, but on 4th November they had to take cover in the school as some of the shelters were full of water.

However, the football team was keeping the spirit of the school high. During the first half of the season they had played twelve matches, won ten, lost one and drawn one. A tea was arranged for the team members before the school closed at Christmas 1940.

The movement of children during these early years of the war was unsettling for pupils and teachers. Children were being evacuated all over the country, a number came to St. Peter's School from areas in the borough of Derby. Many teachers had to go with the children and they were paid 5s (25p) a week for their additional expenses. However many were out of pocket amounting to as much as £20 or £30. The largest majority in the school came from Birmingham, Coventry, London and even East Anglia; a few stayed for only a short time adding to the disruption of school life.

In January 1941 Mr. Maxwell reported to a School Managers' Meeting that accommodation had only been provided for three hundred children in the air raid shelters whereas the number on the Registers was three hundred and seventy. He felt a responsibility for the additional seventy scholars. He further pointed out that children living within five minutes of school might have been sent home but parents had expressed their desire for the children to be kept at school during an air raid therefore he thought the provision of another shelter would meet the case.

The managers were of the opinion that as the average attendance was not the maximum number but about three hundred and forty an additional shelter was not necessary. They also thought that the five-minutes-from-home provision could reasonably be carried out if the children were instructed to take immediate cover in houses on the way home if necessary.

On the night of the April 10th the problem concerning the air raid shelters deteriorated when the middle one of the three on the playing field was hit by a bomb. It happened during the late evening and fortunately, as the warning sirens had not sounded, there was no-one in the shelter. It was October before workmen arrived to build a new shelter but it wasn't completed until December, still awaiting seats which were eventually erected by the scholars.

My sister Sheila's early memories of attending school during the war years was carrying her gas mask on a daily basis and entering the dark air raid shelter situated in the girls' playground. They entered the shelter down the wooden steps, made by the senior boys in their woodwork classes.

After their naval base in Pearl Harbour was attacked on 8th December the United States of America declared war on Japan. Meanwhile events in Britain were dramatically affected by the sinking of the battleships *Prince of Wales* and *Repulse* while on their way to defend Singapore (part of the British Empire) by the Japanese who now occupied Burma. In April Lord Mountbatten was put in charge of combined Allied operations in South East Asia.

A further seventeen children registered at St. Peter's in December. As accommodation in the school was still very tight the headmaster was forced to "promote" other children to higher classes throughout the infants and juniors. He made a comment in the Log Book that these promotions were "uneducational but unavoidable."

None of these children were short-term scholars, the voluntary evacuees allocated to the school at the beginning of the war had all returned to their homes, mostly in the London, Birmingham and Coventry areas.

After school closed the school yard and classrooms were used twice a week by Army Cadets for training classes . The managers agreed that "in the National interest at the present time permission be granted." Blackout conditions were used for the first time in the new block in early in 1942; no doubt the reason for this was that the Youth Club had been given permission to use the school facilities in the evening.

The whole of the school attended a Divine Service in the church on St. Peter's Day, 29th June and at the beginning of July the Board of Education announced that schools, as far as possible, remain open during the summer holidays. The Derbyshire Education Committee asked the managers of the school to decide upon the advisability or otherwise of keeping the school open.

Two important aspects were discussed, the first involving children of parents who were on war work. These amounted to thirty six children with only ten possibly able to attend. The second consideration was the children coming to school for milk and as they only numbered thirty seven, it was decided that the school would close as normal.

Teacher Kenneth George Collier began his first term of employment at St. Peter's on 28th August but had to leave two months later to join the forces. He and Miss Jagg were to play an important part in the education of both my sister Sheila and me throughout our school life.

The recruitment of staff was very difficult throughout the war with main-

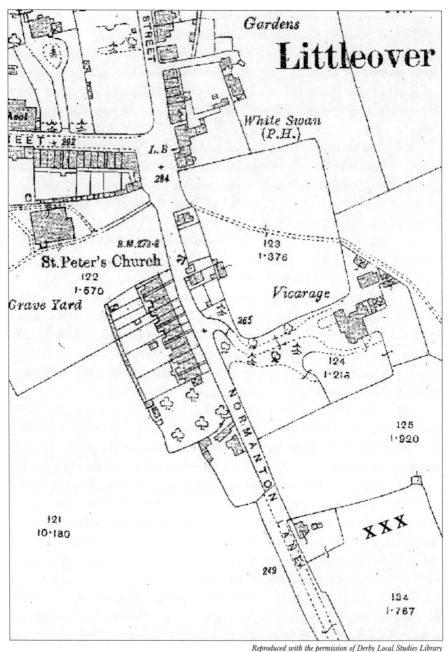

Littleover

Gardens

White Swan
(P.H.)

I.B

284

B.M.273·8

St. Peter's Church
122
1·570

Grave Yard

123
1·376

Vicarage

265

124
1·216

125
1·920

121
10·180

249

XXX

124
1·767

This 1914 Ordnance Survey map shows the position of the school (top left corner) and the playing field (bottom right corner). The X's indicate the position of the air raid shelters.

ly female teachers taking the positions. A youth named Spray arrived from Derby to fill a vacancy but as he had little experience was sent back to the Borough Education Office. There had been a policy of co-operation between the Borough and the County but this appointment proved very unsatisfactory. The County Staff Officer was informed that the headmaster was in charge of the class. Another female certificated assistant, Mrs. Rowley, joined the staff to take over a fortnight later.

The school experienced difficulties keeping the heating up to the recommended temperatures, partly through there being no caretaker from the end of October to March 1943 and partly because of the shortage of fuel. The Sexton of the church took on the duties but in conjunction with other schools in the county the morning sessions commenced later at 9.30 am during the winter months.

There was definitely a more optimistic air in the country as 1942 came to a close. The Beveridge Report recommended a state social insurance "from the cradle to the grave." William Beveridge was an economist whose report formed the basis of the social reform legislation in the forthcoming Labour Government. He also recommended a national health service, family allowances and full-employment policies.

In 1943 the BBC was bringing in more light entertainment programmes, *Desert Island Discs* being broadcast for the first time at the beginning of the year. The School Broadcasting Service also commenced with St. Peter's receiving it towards the end of September.

Hubert Harry Toft, the youngest son of the former head teacher, Benjamin Toft, died on 2nd January 1943, aged 62. He was the organist at Littleover Parish Church. Mr. Maxwell played the organ at his funeral and took over as the Church organist.

The headmaster was not too pleased with some children who had to be sent home for having their hair permanently waved. Mr. Eliott, the School Attendance Officer, was called in to interview them. The welfare regarding employment of children was also taken seriously by the authorities and highlighted by the Superintendent's visit in early 1943 to investigate the absences of four boys who had attended a farm sale on the 14th March. This was soon followed by a call regarding two boys, both under twelve years of age, who were being employed as newspaper boys. The boys had to appear at court in early April due to the prosecution of the newsagent.

School life during 1943 attempted to function on a normal basis despite its continuing accommodation difficulties. It is hard to imagine now, some sixty one years later, but the telephone was installed in the school for the first time in this year.

On 6th January 1944 I should have been starting my first day at school, but for the second year in succession St. Peter's Church School in Littleover was reluctantly unable to admit any infants due to a lack of accommodation.

Unknowingly I was to begin my school life at one of the most radical periods in the history of education. The Board of Education had been discussing educational reconstruction for a number of years and at last they were taking on board many of the recommendations of the Hadow reports commissioned in the 1920s.

The 1944 Education Act introduced by Richard Austen (Rab) Butler raised the school leaving age to fifteen and provided universal free schooling in three different types of secondary schools; grammar, modern and technical.

More than half of the schools were managed by churches, a category which applied to St Peter's. It was understood that they would be unable to finance the modernisation of infant and junior departments. The general agreement was that they should not be abolished but financed under different schemes. If the school was able to meet half the cost of alterations they would become Aided Schools and one third of the managers would be appointed by the local authority.

All these changes took years to implement, the school leaving age came into being in 1947 and St. Peter's was awarded Aided Status in February 1952. At least in March 1944 the Education Minister Rab Butler lifted the unfair ban on women teachers who were being denied work if they married.

Discussion of the radical moves in education had been taking place well before the Bill became law. The Derbyshire Association of Teachers (NUT) met in Derby in February 1944 and expressed concerns about some aspects of the forthcoming Bill such as the need to re-assert the voluntary nature of teachers when supervising school meals. This had remained a problem since school dinners were introduced to the Practising School and others in 1942 (see p114).

A month later the question of staffing was discussed at the Derbyshire

Council of the NUT meeting in Buxton. Mr. Haddock said that thirty seven per cent of teachers were married women or retired teachers, the highest in the country. As staffing in Derbyshire was such an acute problem, the meeting suggested that financial considerations should be given to supplementary teachers and that salaries should be improved overall in line with surrounding areas. Mr. Haddock said that large numbers of extra teachers would be needed under the Bill but he thought that a period of training of less than one year with refresher courses was acceptable.

The Executive of the Derbyshire NUT were able to secure a twenty five per cent increase on the basic scale of pay for uncertificated teachers.

The president of the NUT, E. G. T. Giles, gave his blessing to the Bill when he addressed the Derby Teachers' Association in May. "The Bill was a compromise measure but with all its deficiencies – and there are many – it gave a new conception in outline of an education which could be suitable for the citizens of a great democracy". He went on to warn teachers to be on guard against the faint hearted and the cynics in their own ranks, also to interest parents, especially mothers, in the possibilities which the Bill presented.

A resolution was passed by the Derbyshire Education Committee asking for the return of teachers to their civilian occupation as soon as demobilisation was possible. Suggestions were also to be made to schools that when circulating advice by the Board of Education on sex education, it should be made clear that parents would be allowed to withdraw their children from such instruction.

Allied victory over the German army was more likely at the beginning of 1944 but the most important event for me, on 6th March, was my first journey to school, made less worrying by walking with my sister and other children I knew from Jackson Avenue and surrounding streets.

On reaching the school entrance in Church Street the boys took the first entrance on the west, climbing the stone steps to the playground. Girls walked a little further to the far end of the old schoolrooms, turning into the eastern entrance. Cloakrooms were at both ends of a long corridor and we entered the infants' classrooms on the left, the 1912 extension which overlooked the girls' playground. The girls' and boys' playgrounds were separated by a high brick wall (only its foundation can be seen in the picture on page 51). Between the 1937 classrooms on the north and the old schoolrooms on Church Street there was the toilet block, built in 1912. This was disliked by myself and my contemporaries, mainly for its age and lack of privacy than for being unhygienic.

The domestic science room in the new building was closed and used as an additional classroom on the day I started school. The layout in the old school building became familiar within a very short time. I was amazed on my return nearly sixty years later to see similar windows looking out onto Church Street and the wooden cupboard which must have survived from those installed in 1913. The two partitions have gone and it is now one long classroom but the fittings are still visible.

Public complaints were made that political leaders both locally and nationally had "dangled education improvements" in front of the public before facilities could be provided. This led to some parental disappointment.

A deputation of a hundred and twenty residents of Littleover attended the Parish Council meeting in

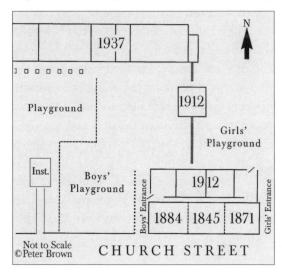

May 1944, demanding the immediate provision of secondary education in Littleover as inadequate places were being allotted to county children in borough schools. The deputation felt that a building could be taken over, not necessarily in the centre of Littleover, travelling expenses would not be objected to. The Chairman of the Council, Mr. A. H. Barnacle was in full sympathy but pointed out that if a building was used on a temporary basis it was doubtful if the necessary equipment or staff could be provided at that time. Councillor Knee suggested the deputation should ascertain how many children in the parish desired to obtain secondary education and submit the figures to the local MP. In the long term all this proved to be academic, for on 10th January 1949 Littleover County Secondary School on Pastures Hill opened; the first newly built Secondary Modern School to be built in Derbyshire.

The modern interior of the building extension built in 1912, overlooking what was the girls' playground in the 1940s.

The interior of the east end of the classroom the 1871 extension. The window overlooked the girls' entrance when the author started school. The cupboard at the far end has been in this room since 1913.

St Peter's School re-opened after the Whitsuntide holiday, the day before the Normandy landings on June 6th, when 156,000 men were sent in a huge invasion fleet across the English Channel to relieve Europe from German occupation. A month later the school was used as a rest centre for the reception of mothers and children who had been evacuated from London because of the dangers from flying V-bombs. These were small jet-propelled pilotless aircraft, also called flying or buzz bombs, targeted by the Germans on London from sites in northern France and Holland. They caused considerable damage and loss of life at first but the RAF was later able to shoot them down over the sea.

There were fifty four evacuees in the school from early July. This presented further strains on the staff and accommodation along with examinations and end of term requirements. Miss Schofield was sent by the London City Council to help on a temporary basis at the end of July. The majority of the evacuees returned to London after three months, a few having to stay because of a loss of home or family during the bombing.

At a school managers' meeting in September Dr Watt reported that plans for the erection of a school canteen had been passed. No communication had been received from the

The author's first school photograph.

Education Committee as it was not one of their priorities. The plan was to site the canteen to the west of the new school block.

A group of six girls, due to leave school, were taken to Rowley's Hosiery Manufacturers in London Road, Derby by Miss Jagg and six boys accompanied the headmaster on a visit to Clarke's Aircraft Products factory. The boys were shown all the stages of production and allowed to inspect the machines. The headmaster reported in the Log Book that "the visit was most useful and helped to correct some erroneous impressions that had been gained prior to the visit." This arrangement of visiting local employers became an annual event until St. Peter's became a junior school in 1948.

Complaints were received about the behaviour of boys on buses and trespassing on the private property of Dr Watt in November. He lived at the Walnuts, just off Littleover Hollow. The headmaster again makes a concise entry in the Log Book on 9th November. "The two matters were emphatically dealt with at school assembly this morning."

Permission was granted by the Director of Education for the school to close for Christmas at 12 noon on December 22nd, my birthday, what a bonus! The school re-opened on 8th January 1945 with new admissions being registered at the beginning of the year for the first time in three years.

Although this was the centenary year of St. Peter's School, events in Europe were overtaking any self congratulation. In April British troops liberated the people in the Belsen concentration camp; the blackout in London came to an end; Mussolini, the Italian dictator was shot and Adolph Hitler committed suicide. By 8th May (twelve days before the original 1845 Trust Deed for the school land was signed), the end of the war against Germany was officially declared.

The school was closed for the next two days in honour of Victory in Europe, today known as "VE Day".

No official celebrations were organised at the school but this is not surprising as the British Government had only announced an unconditional surrender at 3.00 pm on 8th May and then hours later confirming a public holiday for the following day. It was left for everyone to organise their own street parties. There were at least school Christmas concerts and parties to look forward to for the children.

Two years later, on 25th July 1947, the headmaster, Mr. Thomas Maxwell, left the school to take up a similar post at Tamworth Road County School, Long Eaton. He was presented with a refectory table and an engraved fountain pen and pencil by the staff, and pupils. As well as his other interests in music Mr. Maxwell had been the musical director of the Derby Opera Company. A recording of three songs by the school choir, conducted by Mr. G. H. Heath Gracie, organist and choirmaster at Derby Cathedral, was played at his retirement presentations. Mr. Maxwell was followed by Mr. Thomas Whitehall who was teaching at Allenton Senior Boys' School. He too continued what was becoming a tradition at St. Peter's, a

The staff at St Peter's School, photographed in late 1947 or early 1948. Top row left to right. Florence Millward?, Mrs Bishop, unknown, Alfred Stanton, Kenneth Collier, Hilda Brown?, Marjorie Marriott, unknown, William Anderson?, Alice Singleton, Winifred Jagg, Thomas Whitehall (Headmaster), Thomas Whittingham, Bertha Turner, John Grundy.

great interest in music. Since 1936 Mr. Whitehall had been a member of Derby Cathedral Choir and was a conductor with Derby and County Grand Opera Company. He was to retire after twenty seven years.

My memorable experiences at St. Peter's and the years spent at Littleover County Secondary School, Pastures Hill, as it was then called, are told in a further book *Mickleover Born & Bred*. The continuing history of St. Peter's will hopefully be told by another ex pupil sometime in the future.

CHAPTER SIX

HOW TIMES HAVE CHANGED

2004 Onwards

Who would have imagined the progression of education in Littleover since schooling began some one hundred and sixty years ago. In the days when children were taught monotonous subjects by copying lessons onto black pieces of slate by means of chalk sticks.

The first progression was the coming of the Education Act in 1870, promoted by forward thinking government inspectors such as Matthew Arnold. The greatest progression, as far as St. Peter's is concerned, was the appointment of dedicated headmasters, beginning with Benjamin Toft in 1870. All of them in the first hundred years of the school were strict disciplinarians who used corporal punishment which at that time was not breaking the law.

The health of the children along with physical exercise became paramount in the first quarter of the twentieth century although a school canteen was only in the planning stage when I began my school life in 1944. The majority of children walked home for lunch and returned to school in time for afternoon lessons. Those of us living in Jackson Avenue had a two mile journey overall and I was only six years old.

The big discussions taking place at St. Peter's today are whether to allow children to bring mobile phones into the school, the main argument in favour is for their own personal safety.

As an Aided Church of England Junior School the Christian faith is still taught along with other faiths and cultures. The church still owns the site and buildings as it always has. However, managing the school has changed, as St Peter's Church congregation no longer hold all the seats on the committee with the Vicar acting as the Chairman. The Church Governors do have a majority on the Governing Body but the Chair has been appointed from another church in the Diocese.

Head Teacher Shaun Miles began his career at St. Peter's in September 2001 and is supported by Mrs. N. Clark and eight fully qualified teachers, overseeing just over two hundred and fifty registered pupils.

Not all the costs of maintaining the school are met by the Education Authority and as in the past, parents accepted some responsibility for raising school funds. Today it is called the "Barchester Fund". A small donation per annum is given by the parents to cover the necessary premiums in maintaining the buildings of the school along with the insurance.

St. Peter's recognises the need to enhance the quality of education and invests heavily in information technology as it is now a core aspect of the National Curriculum. A designated ITC Suite has been built in front of the 1937 school extension. It was opened by the Bishop of Derby, The Rt. Revd. Jonathan Bailey on September 18th 2003. Interactive whiteboards are now installed in every classroom in the school at a cost of £24,000 which was allocated in the annual budget. The boards use the latest advances in digital electromagnetic sensing technology. This requires a computer, a projector and a wall mounted whiteboard. The computer image is controlled by the teacher or children touching the board directly or by using a special pen.

Head teacher, Shaun Miles envisages the children having links with other schools in the future, allowing them to see and talk to people from all over the world as though they were sitting in the classroom. The school web site is also interactive.

Headteacher, Shaun Miles and his staff are proud of the investment made by the school in modern technology.

Shaun Miles addresses the school at the final assembly before Easter 2004. The hall was built in 1962. The far end occupies the land where the Institute one stood.

St. Peter's is also part of the Derby City Network Learning Community whereby schools in Derby are able to go and look at the strengths and techniques of others and bring them back to Littleover.

As in days past the head teacher is still very much involved in how the school operates on a daily basis. Shaun sees himself as the resident inspector in the school and takes an overview of its strengths and weaknesses.

There is a pupil school council at St. Peter's where the children have a say in how the school is run. Each class has two representatives and they are referred to as councillors at their regular meetings. Two examples of changes by the children through talks and discussions with the head teacher have been in the toilets and dining room. The children chose the decorating scheme. The dining room was also given new paintwork, using the Harry Potter theme which the children much appreciated and proved they have a choice.

I know from the period I spent at the school going through material, that the children are very happy, self-assured and confident, showing respect to each other and the members of the staff. The school can feel proud of its achievements and radical plans for the future. Shaun Miles hopes to shape citizens of tomorrow who may become future leaders with all having a place in society. He ends. "We have got to make sure we give them the chance to find their strengths and confidence to progress in whatever field they choose." I am sure St Peter's is in good and caring hands and will go on to reach its second century with the same pride as it did in reaching the first.

The author shares the interest of Year 5 pupils looking at one of the old logbooks in the oldest classroom at the school.

CONCLUSION

This book is left to end in something of an anti-climax. I have little to report on my experiences over the first twenty-two months of my school life but judged over the following five years I cannot say that I was inspired by any particular teacher. My early reports show that I was above average on most subjects but lacking drive in others which, on the whole, is a fair assessment of my efforts. I do remember a mostly pleasurable interlude in my life spent at St Peter's, particularly the company and friendship of other children. As with many of us I began to "shine", if that's the correct term, after leaving school. I was fortunate in entering a trade which I loved from the day I began; an apprenticeship in the newspaper trade. From the knowledge and experience I gained over a number of years I became capable to run my own business for more than twenty years, so the groundwork that enabled me to achieve this must partly go back to my time at St Peter's School and the skill of the teachers at the time. It was not all their fault that some of their teaching fell on deaf ears and uninspired grey cells.

Perhaps the best judgement of the school we can rely on in the middle 1940s is the HMI's report of his visit on 14th and 18th March 1946.

> In spite of a modern extension of buildings to house the top classes, the school is still inadequately accommodated. It has no hall and no dining hall. In consequence the children are deprived of Physical Training in bad weather and the activities proper to a school of this type are necessarily curtailed through lack of facilities. It has not been found possible to arrange a school dinner, a fact which bears hardly on a proportion of the children who live at a fair distance from the school. A more serious handicap particularly to work in the Senior classes is caused by the necessity for using the Domestic Science and Crafts room in the new building as a classroom. There is, in consequence, no Domestic Science teaching for the girls though the boys have Woodwork instruction in a local centre.

> The staff includes five married women teachers who returned to teaching after a long absence to replace the men on war service. They have served the school extremely well during the war years and are to be congratulated on the standards they have maintained in a large all-age school of this type. It is desirable now, however, that the headteacher should have, as soon as possible, the help of one or more experienced men teachers if justice is to be done to the Senior classes, particularly the boys of 12 to 14.

> In spite of the difficulties of accommodation and the lack of a hall, the school is well organised and the work schemes well thought out. The headteacher has

done good work in directing and controlling his school and in building up a very real school spirit.

The children are given an excellent start in the Infant classes, particularly in the first year, where the responsibility rests with a teacher of very long experience whose work is notably good. There is an atmosphere of happy purposeful activity in these first two years and a firm foundation is laid for the Junior School work.

The work in the Junior classes, although quite satisfactory in attainment, would be more valuable if the staff demanded a greater contribution of serious independent effort from the children. The children for the most part come from good class homes and the average ability is fairly high. There is however a tendency to shirk tasks which require steady persistent efforts and independent thought and action, with the result that the work was a certain easy superficiality. It is important that this tendency should be corrected before the children reach the Senior classes. This can only be done by giving them more solid fare in the way of problems to tackle and tasks to be completed. In short, their ability and background are such that they should be extended and encouraged to offer sustained individual effort in their work rather than to take the easy road of absorbing sufficient superficial knowledge to satisfy the demand of the syllabus.

It is in the top classes that the results of this weakness in the Junior School are seen. There is here a noticeably passive attitude to the work which is rather disappointing after the excellent beginning in the lower classes. It is true that the top classes have been drastically "creamed", not only by a quite substantial entry to Secondary Grammar School but also, at this school, by a real effort both mental and physical if they are to escape the feeling of inferiority which leads to listlessness. Much could be done if more attention were given in the work of leavers in their last term. It should be possible to set every leaver a goal to be reached and to stimulate his individual efforts by giving him a definite assignment in accordance with his capabilities.

These observations are made not as a criticism of the standard of work being done at present. This is quite satisfactory generally and in Music and Art it is above the normal average. It is felt however that a school of this type could now go forward towards the establishment of a real Secondary Modern education in its top classes. The present headteacher and staff, strengthened by the return of one or possibly two experienced men teachers are quite capable of making this progress.

No evidence remains of what the headmaster and teachers thought of this report, but it is known that those in the profession at that time were very critical of some of the inspectors.

TEACHERS AT ST. PETER'S SCHOOL

(Who have been at the school more twelve months or more)

Full Name of Teacher	Qualification if Known	Date Started if Known	Date Left if Known
Thomas Richards		? 1866	?April 1869
Benjamin Toft (Head)	Certificated	7 Mar 1870	31 Aug 1905
Mrs Toft		7 Mar 1870	31 Aug 1905
Sarah Gilman	Pupil Teacher	August 1876	March 1881
Annie Mary Toft	Certificated	1 Feb 1877	27 July 1928
Edith Martha Toft	Certificated	1 Feb 1885	26 June 1918
Bryan Daykin (Head)	Certificated	1 Sept 1905	31 Dec 1931
Annie Daykin, Mrs		27 Aug 1906	31 Dec 1931
Katherine Jerrome	Certificated	1 Oct 1906	31 July 1914
Became Mrs. Heath	Supply Teacher		
Ethel Daykin	Student	1 Aug 1911	? 1913
Eva Margaret Phillips	Student	21 Aug 1911	? 1913
Eva Isabel Bryan	Assistant	1 Nov 1913	31 Aug 1933
Horace Reginald Riley	Certificated	28 Aug 1916	19 April 1918
Florence Verena Elliott		5 July 1918	31 Dec 1920
Gladys Mabel Kidger	Certificated	11 July 1921	23 Feb 1923
Doris Isabel Garratt	Certificated	1 Nov 1923	27 July 1928
Frances Bertha Jackson	Certificated	27 Aug 1928	24 Aug 1942
Kathleen May Lockwood	Uncertificated	27 Aug 1928	16 Oct 1928
Mary Elizabeth Reeve		17 Oct 1928	13 April 1931
Bertha Juliette Hudson	Uncertificated	8 Sept 1931	16 Feb 1933
Robert Noble	Uncertificated	1 Feb 1932	31 Aug 1933
Thomas Maxwell (Head)	Certificated	1 Mar 1932	25 July 1947 ·
Ivan Ward	Certificated	21 Aug 1933	30 Aug 1935

Full Name of Teacher	Qualification if Known	Date Started if Known	Date Left if Known
Madge Spencer	Uncertificated	1 Mar 1934	21 Sept 1934
" "		19 Oct 1936	28 Feb 1939
Freda Mary Tunnicliffe	Certificated	16 Oct 1934	24 Dec 1937
Hugh Whitaker	Certificated	1 Sept 1935	2 April 1938
" "		27 Mar 1939	28 Aug 1942
Lizzie Grattidge	Uncertificated	1 Nov 1936	8 Mar 1940
Ronald Alexander Davies	Certificated	? April 1937	31 Aug 1938
Annie Irene Lenton	Certificated	15 Aug 1938	31 July 1939
*Donald Grist	Certificated	19 Sept 1938	21 May 1940
" "		15 April 1946	31 Oct 1946
*Thomas Edward Whittingham	Certificated	15 Aug 1938	19 Sept 1938
" " "		15 April 1946	30 Mar 1952
Mr. J. R. Banks	Certificated	? Sept 1938	24 Jan 1940
Winifred Mary Jagg	Certificated	30 Sept 1940	22 Dec 1948
Alice L. Singleton (Mrs.)	Certificated	5 Mar 1940	29 Aug 1952
Miss G. Idill	Uncertificated	1 June 1940	24 Dec 1942
Muriel Norma Williams (Mrs.)	Certificated	1 Aug 1939	2 Aug 1946
Mrs E. Lownes		? July 1940	24 Aug 1942
Margaret Elizabeth Huxley	Certificated	24 Aug 1942	29 Mar 1945
*Kenneth George Collier	Assistant	25 Aug 1942	30 Oct 1942
" " "		2 Sept 1946	31 Aug 1949
Mrs Rowley	Certificated	16 Sept 1942	16 Apr 1946
Mrs Orme		19 Jan 1943	16 Apr 1946
Gladys Mary Adlington	Certificated	1 Sept 1943	31 Jan 1946
Marjorie Pattie Marriott	Certificated	27 Mar 1944	19 July 1962

These teachers were called up to joined HM Services in World War Two.

BIBLIOGRAPHY

1870-1970 Century Growth in English Education – By H. C. Dent,
Longman 1970

A History of Western Education Vol 3 – By James Bowen, Methuen 1981
Archives:
Derby Local Studies Library, Irongate, Derby
Derbyshire Record Office, Matlock, Derbyshire
The Magic Attic, Swadlincote, South Derbyshire

Britain in the Era of Two World Wars 1914-1945 – Andrew Thorpe
Longman 1994

Directory of Derbyshire 1846, Bagshaw

Education and Economic Decline in Britain 1870 to the 1990s –
By Michael Sanderson, Cambridge University Press 1999

History of the Second World War (Vol 1 - 6), Purnell 1966

Inside Primary School – John Blackie, HMSO 1967

Littleover and Its Church – A. B. Scott, 1916

Littleover Portrait of a Village – Ian Griffiths, 1990

Mickleover & Littleover, a History –
by Susan Watson, Watnay Publishing 1993

Newspapers:
Derby Evening Telegraph
Derbyshire Advertiser
Derby Mercury
Derby Daily Graphic

St. Peter's Church of England School:
Admission Registers
Log Books
Photograph Collection
Minute Books of Board of Managers,
October 1925 - November 1948

Theory & Practice in the New Secondary Schools –
By A. Greenhough & F. A. Crofts, University of London Press 1949

The Great World War (Vol. IV), Gresham Publishing 1920

The Welfare State – Derek Fraser, Sutton 2000

CORRIGENDA

"The Pastures" on Rykneld Road does not survive as a hospital
as stated on page 5. This closed in 1994 and has been
converted into the Independent Grammar School for Boys.
The reference to *The Education of the Adolescent* of 1916 on page
81 is wrongly printed. The date should have read 1926.